D1581798

526 705 97 0

ENGLISH
FOR EVERYONE

COURSE BOOK LEVEL 2
BUSINESS ENGLISH

 FREE AUDIO
website and app
www.dkefe.com

Author

Victoria Boobyer is a freelance writer, presenter, and teacher trainer with a background in English-language teaching and teacher management. She has a keen interest in the use of graded readers and the sound pedagogical use of technology in teaching.

Course consultant

Tim Bowen has taught English and trained teachers in more than 30 countries worldwide. He is the co-author of works on pronunciation teaching and language-teaching methodology, and author of numerous books for English-language teachers. He is currently a freelance materials writer, editor, and translator. He is a member of the Chartered Institute of Linguists.

Language consultant

Professor Susan Barduhn is an experienced English-language teacher, teacher trainer, and author, who has contributed to numerous publications. In addition to directing English-language courses in at least four different continents, she has been President of the International Association of Teachers of English as a Foreign Language, and an adviser to the British Council and the US State Department. She is currently a Professor at the School of International Training in Vermont, USA.

ENGLISH FOR EVERYONE

COURSE BOOK LEVEL ❷

BUSINESS ENGLISH

Project Editors Lili Bryant, Laura Sandford
Art Editors Chrissy Barnard, Paul Drislane, Michelle Staples
Editor Ben Ffrancon Davies
Editorial Assistants Sarah Edwards, Helen Leech
Illustrators Edwood Burn, Michael Parkin, Gus Scott
Managing Editor Daniel Mills
Managing Art Editor Anna Hall
Audio Recording Manager Christine Stroyan
Jacket Designer Ira Sharma
Jacket Editor Claire Gell
Managing Jacket Editor Saloni Singh
Jacket Design Development Manager Sophia MTT
Producer, Pre-production Andy Hilliard
Producer Mary Slater
Publisher Andrew Macintyre
Art Director Karen Self
Publishing Director Jonathan Metcalf

DK India
Senior Managing Art Editor Arunesh Talapatra
Senior Art Editor Chhaya Sajwan
Art Editors Meenal Goel, Roshni Kapur
Assistant Art Editor Rohit Dev Bhardwaj
Illustrators Manish Bhatt, Arun Pottirayil,
Sachin Tanwar, Mohd Zishan
Editorial Coordinator Priyanka Sharma
Pre-production Manager Balwant Singh
Senior DTP Designers Harish Aggarwal, Vishal Bhatia
DTP Designer Jaypal Chauhan

First published in Great Britain in 2017 by
Dorling Kindersley Limited
80 Strand, London, WC2R 0RL

Copyright © 2017 Dorling Kindersley Limited
A Penguin Random House Company
10 8 6 4 2 1 3 5 7 9
001–296905–Jan/2017

All rights reserved.
No part of this publication may be reproduced, stored
in or introduced into a retrieval system, or transmitted,
in any form, or by any means (electronic, mechanical,
photocopying, recording, or otherwise), without the prior
written permission of the copyright owner.

A CIP catalogue record for this book
is available from the British Library.
ISBN: 978-0-2412-7514-6

Printed and bound in China

A WORLD OF IDEAS:
SEE ALL THERE IS TO KNOW

www.dk.com

Contents

How the course works

English for Everyone is designed for people who want to teach themselves the English language. The Business English edition covers essential English phrases and constructions for a wide range of common business scenarios. Unlike other courses, *English for Everyone* uses images and graphics in all its learning and practice, to help you understand and remember as easily as possible. The best way to learn is to work through the book in order, making full use of the audio available on the website and app. Turn to the practice book at the end of each unit to reinforce your learning with additional exercises.

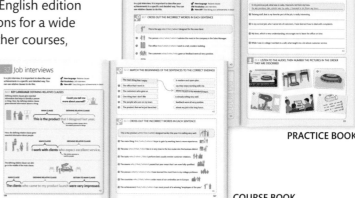

PRACTICE BOOK

COURSE BOOK

Unit number The book is divided into units. The unit number helps you keep track of your progress.

Learning points Every unit begins with a summary of the key learning points.

Modules Each unit is broken down into modules, which should be done in order. You can take a break from learning after completing any module.

Language learning Modules with colored backgrounds teach new language points. Study these carefully before moving on to the exercises.

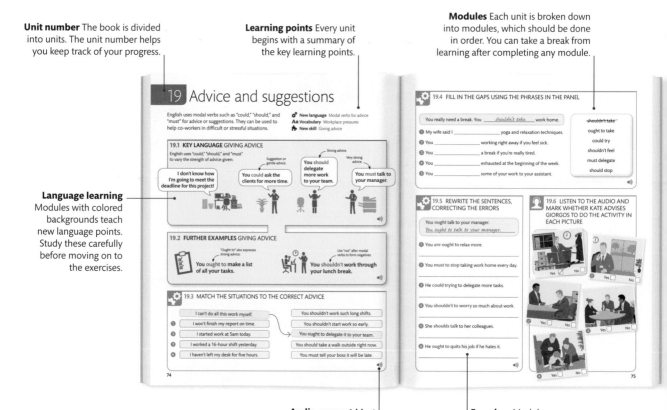

Audio support Most modules are supported by audio recordings to help you improve your speaking and listening skills.

Exercises Modules with white backgrounds contain exercises that help you practice your new skills to reinforce learning.

FREE AUDIO
website and app
www.dkefe.com

Language modules

New language is shown in the context of common business scenarios. Each learning module introduces appropriate English for a particular situation, as well as general points of English language to improve your overall fluency.

Module number Every module is identified with a unique number, so you can track your progress and easily locate any related audio.

Module heading The teaching topic appears here, along with a brief introduction.

Graphic guide Clear, simple visuals help to explain the meaning of new language forms, and show you business situations in which you might expect to use them.

Sample language New language points are introduced in common business contexts. Colored highlights make new constructions easy to spot, and annotations explain them.

Supporting audio This symbol indicates that the model sentences featured in the module are available as audio recordings.

Formation guide Visual guides break down English grammar into its simplest parts, showing you how to recreate even complex formations.

Vocabulary Throughout the book, vocabulary modules list the most common and useful English words and phrases for business, with visual cues to help you remember them.

Write-on lines You are encouraged to write your own translations of English words to create your own reference pages.

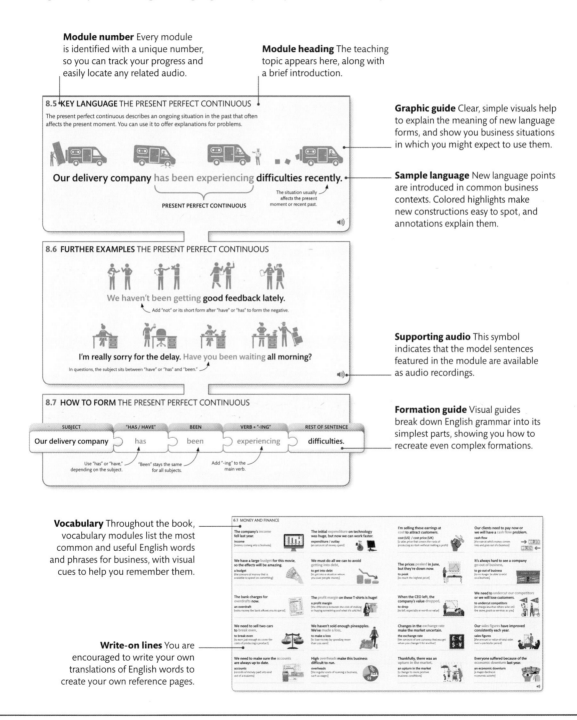

8.5 KEY LANGUAGE THE PRESENT PERFECT CONTINUOUS

The present perfect continuous describes an ongoing situation in the past that often affects the present moment. You can use it to offer explanations for problems.

Our delivery company has been experiencing difficulties recently.

PRESENT PERFECT CONTINUOUS

The situation usually affects the present moment or recent past.

8.6 FURTHER EXAMPLES THE PRESENT PERFECT CONTINUOUS

We haven't been getting good feedback lately.

Add "not" or its short form after "have" or "has" to form the negative.

I'm really sorry for the delay. Have you been waiting all morning?

In questions, the subject sits between "have" or "has" and "been."

8.7 HOW TO FORM THE PRESENT PERFECT CONTINUOUS

SUBJECT	"HAS / HAVE"	BEEN	VERB + "-ING"	REST OF SENTENCE
Our delivery company	has	been	experiencing	difficulties.

Use "has" or "have," depending on the subject.

"Been" stays the same for all subjects.

Add "-ing" to the main verb.

Practice modules

Each learning point is followed by carefully graded exercises that help to fix new language in your memory. Working through the exercises will help you remember what you have learned and become more fluent. Every exercise is introduced with a symbol to indicate which skill is being practiced.

 GRAMMAR
Apply new language rules in different contexts.

 READING
Examine target language in real-life English contexts.

 LISTENING
Test your understanding of spoken English.

 VOCABULARY
Cement your understanding of key vocabulary.

WRITING
Practice producing written passages of English text.

SPEAKING
Compare your spoken English to model audio recordings.

Module number Every module is identified with a unique number, so you can easily locate answers and related audio.

Exercise instruction Every exercise is introduced with a brief instruction, telling you what you need to do.

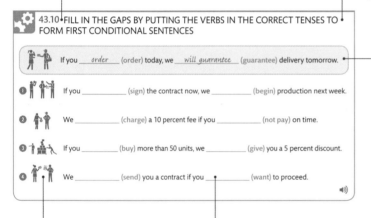

43.10 FILL IN THE GAPS BY PUTTING THE VERBS IN THE CORRECT TENSES TO FORM FIRST CONDITIONAL SENTENCES

If you ___order___ (order) today, we ___will guarantee___ (guarantee) delivery tomorrow.

1 If you _____ (sign) the contract now, we _____ (begin) production next week.

2 We _____ (charge) a 10 percent fee if you _____ (not pay) on time.

3 If you _____ (buy) more than 50 units, we _____ (give) you a 5 percent discount.

4 We _____ (send) you a contract if you _____ (want) to proceed.

Sample answer The first question of each exercise is answered for you, to help make the task easy to understand.

Supporting graphics Visual cues are given to help you understand the exercises.

Space for writing You are encouraged to write your answers in the book for future reference.

8.4 CROSS OUT THE INCORRECT WORD IN EACH SENTENCE, THEN SAY THE SENTENCES OUT LOUD

I'm sorry / ~~much~~ about the delay.

1 We'll see / look into the problem for you.

2 We'll give / giving you a discount voucher.

3 Could you hold the phone / line a moment?

4 Let's see what / when we can do.

Speaking exercise This symbol indicates that you should say your answers out loud, then compare them to model recordings included in your audio files.

Listening exercise This symbol indicates that you should listen to an audio track in order to answer the questions in the exercise.

Supporting audio This symbol shows that the answers to the exercise are available as audio tracks. Listen to them after completing the exercise.

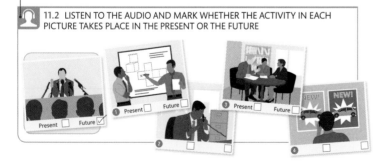

11.2 LISTEN TO THE AUDIO AND MARK WHETHER THE ACTIVITY IN EACH PICTURE TAKES PLACE IN THE PRESENT OR THE FUTURE

Present □ Future ☑

1 Present □ Future □

3 Present □ Future □

2 □

4 □

Audio

English for Everyone features extensive supporting audio materials. You are encouraged to use them as much as you can, to improve your understanding of spoken English, and to make your own accent and pronunciation more natural. Each file can be played, paused, and repeated as often as you like, until you are confident you understand what has been said.

LISTENING EXERCISES
This symbol indicates that you should listen to an audio track in order to answer the questions in the exercise.

SUPPORTING AUDIO
This symbol indicates that extra audio material is available for you to listen to after completing the module.

FREE AUDIO
website and app
www.dkefe.com

Track your progress

The course is designed to make it easy to monitor your progress, with regular summary and review modules. Answers are provided for every exercise, so you can see how well you have understood each teaching point.

Checklists Every unit ends with a checklist, where you can check off the new skills you have learned.

05 ✓ CHECKLIST
⚙️ Modal verbs for obligation ☐ Aa Delegation and politeness ☐ ➕ Delegating tasks to colleagues ☐

Review modules At the end of a group of units, you will find a more detailed review module, summarizing the language you have learned.

Check boxes Use these boxes to mark the skills you feel comfortable with. Go back and review anything you feel you need to practice further.

32

32.2 ◄))
❶ The office that I work in **is modern and open-plan**.
❷ The customers who gave us **feedback were all very positive**.
❸ One thing that I don't like **about my job is the long hours**.
❹ The people who are on my team **say they enjoy working with me**.
❺ The product that we've just launched **is already selling very well**.

32.3 ◄))
❶ The main thing **that** I hope to gain by working here is more experience.
❷ The area **that** I live in is very close to the bus routes into the business district.
❸ The tasks **that** I perform best usually involve customer relations.
❹ The exams **that** I passed last year mean that I am now fully qualified.
❺ The person **who** I have learned the most from is my college professor.
❻ The countries **that** order most of our umbrellas are in Europe.
❼ The achievement **that** I am most proud of is winning "employee of the year."

32.5 ◄))
❶ I have completed all the training, **which** means you wouldn't need to train me.
❷ My boss, **who** is very talented, always encourages me not to work too late.
❸ IT development, **which** is my favorite part of the job, is very fast-paced.
❹ My co-workers, who are all older than me, have taught me a lot.
❺ I worked at the reception desk, **which** taught me how to deal with customers.
❻ I take my job very seriously, which means I always follow the company dress code.
❼ In my last job, **which** was in Paris, I learned to speak French fluently.

Answers Find the answers to every exercise printed at the back of the book.

Exercise numbers Match these numbers to the unique identifier at the top-left corner of each exercise.

Audio This symbol indicates that the answers can also be listened to.

REVIEW THE ENGLISH YOU HAVE LEARNED IN UNITS 1–5

NEW LANGUAGE	SAMPLE SENTENCE	☑	UNIT
INTRODUCING YOURSELF AND OTHERS	You must be Eric from the UK. Tony, this is Hayao from our Japanese office.	☐	1.1
THE PAST SIMPLE AND THE PAST CONTINUOUS FOR PAST EXPERIENCES	I was working 60 hours per week when I came here.	☐	2.1
THE PAST TENSE FOR POLITENESS	Did you want a tour of the office?	☐	2.4
TALKING ABOUT THE RECENT PAST WITH THE PRESENT PERFECT SIMPLE	I have worked in a few different teams.	☐	2.6
TALKING ABOUT CHANGES WITH "USED TO" AND "BE / GET USED TO"	Staff used to eat lunch at their desks. It took a while to get used to the commute.	☐	4.1
	I have to leave this with you. Could you look after this for me?	☐	5.1, 5.6

01 Introductions

When you first join a company, there are many phrases that you can use to introduce yourself. Other people may also use a variety of phrases to introduce you.

⚙️ **New language** Present simple and continuous
Aa Vocabulary Etiquette for introductions
🧩 **New skill** Introducing yourself and others

1.1 KEY LANGUAGE INTRODUCING YOURSELF AND OTHERS

It is common to shake hands with new colleagues and introduce yourself.

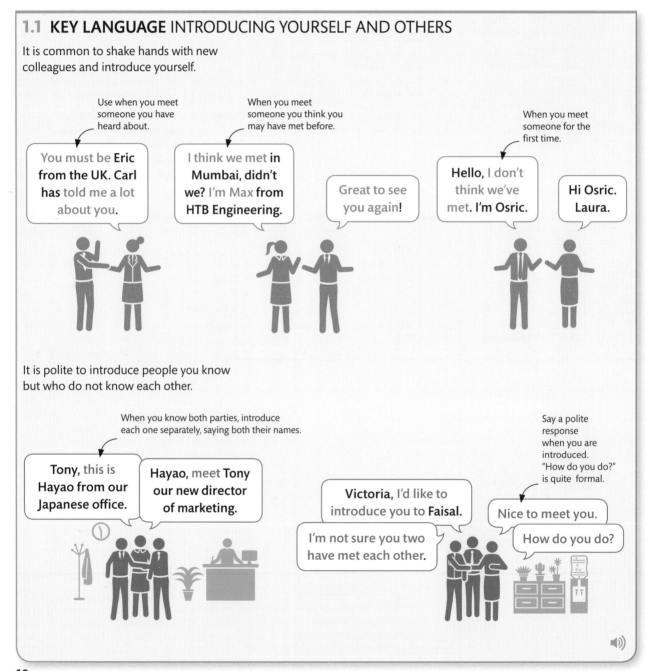

Use when you meet someone you have heard about.

You must be Eric from the UK. Carl has told me a lot about you.

When you meet someone you think you may have met before.

I think we met in Mumbai, didn't we? I'm Max from HTB Engineering.

Great to see you again!

When you meet someone for the first time.

Hello, I don't think we've met. I'm Osric.

Hi Osric. Laura.

It is polite to introduce people you know but who do not know each other.

When you know both parties, introduce each one separately, saying both their names.

Tony, this is Hayao from our Japanese office.

Hayao, meet Tony our new director of marketing.

Victoria, I'd like to introduce you to Faisal.

I'm not sure you two have met each other.

Say a polite response when you are introduced. "How do you do?" is quite formal.

Nice to meet you.

How do you do?

1.2 MATCH THE BEGINNINGS OF THE INTRODUCTIONS TO THE CORRECT ENDINGS

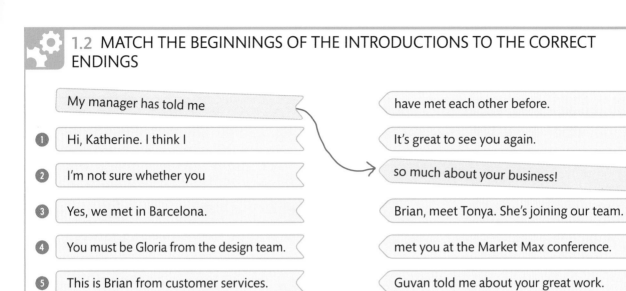

My manager has told me — so much about your business!

1 Hi, Katherine. I think I

2 I'm not sure whether you

3 Yes, we met in Barcelona.

4 You must be Gloria from the design team.

5 This is Brian from customer services.

have met each other before.

It's great to see you again.

so much about your business!

Brian, meet Tonya. She's joining our team.

met you at the Market Max conference.

Guvan told me about your great work.

1.3 FILL IN THE GAPS USING THE WORDS IN THE PANEL

You _____ *must* _____ be Joe Smith.

1 Did we _____ at a conference?

2 Really good to _____ you again.

3 Roula, meet Maria, _____ new assistant.

4 I'd like to _____ you to Karl.

5 Have you two _____ each other before?

~~must~~	introduce
meet	our
met	see

1.4 LISTEN TO THE AUDIO AND ANSWER THE QUESTIONS

Delegates at a conference are introducing themselves.

Jared has met Sasha before.
True ✓ **False** ☐ **Not given** ☐

1 Jared works in the Lima office.
True ☐ **False** ☐ **Not given** ☐

2 Daniel and Sasha have not met before.
True ☐ **False** ☐ **Not given** ☐

3 Daniel shares an office with Jared.
True ☐ **False** ☐ **Not given** ☐

4 Their new product is expensive.
True ☐ **False** ☐ **Not given** ☐

5 Sasha works in Lima.
True ☐ **False** ☐ **Not given** ☐

1.5 KEY LANGUAGE THE PRESENT SIMPLE AND THE PRESENT CONTINUOUS

The present simple is used to describe something that happens in general, or is part of a routine. The present continuous describes something that is happening right now, and will be continuing for a limited time.

I don't usually enjoy networking, but I'm enjoying this conference.

Present simple is the same as the base form of the verb without "to."

Present continuous is formed by adding "be" before the verb and "-ing" to the verb.

 ## 1.6 READ THE ARTICLE AND ANSWER THE QUESTIONS

What word is used for making connections?
Networking ☑ **Sharing** ☐ **Dividing** ☐

1 What kind of people is the article aimed at?
Shy ☐ **Confident** ☐ **Intelligent** ☐

2 What types of connections are useful?
New ones ☐ **Good ones** ☐ **Lots of them** ☐

3 Who might be useful people to talk to?
Ex-colleagues ☐ **Recruiters** ☐ **Family** ☐

4 What do shy people do a lot?
Lie ☐ **Say sorry** ☐ **Say thank you** ☐

5 What does apologizing a lot make you seem?
Confident ☐ **Worried** ☐ **Unprofessional** ☐

6 Where should you look when talking to people?
Their eyes ☐ **Their feet** ☐ **Their mouths** ☐

7 What should you give contacts?
Money ☐ **Gifts** ☐ **Your business card** ☐

CAREER LADDER

Making connections

How to network better if you're shy

Networking doesn't necessarily mean talking to hundreds of people at a conference. A few good connections are much better than meeting lots of people who you will never hear from again. Start by chatting to ex-colleagues or old friends. Ask what they are doing now and share your experiences.

One common habit of shy people is to constantly apologize for everything. Apologizing all of the time looks unprofessional and shows a lack of confidence in yourself. Instead of saying sorry, remember to smile, maintain eye contact, ask questions, and, of course, exchange business cards.

1.7 REWRITE THE SENTENCES, CORRECTING THE ERRORS

> I am being happy to finally meet you, Zoe.
> *I'm happy to finally meet you, Zoe.*

1 Hi James. I'm Vanisha. I don't think we are meeting before.

_____

2 Ashley, I'd like introduce you to my colleague Neil.

_____

3 I enjoying the presentations. Are you?

_____

4 Nice to meet you Bethany. How do you doing?

_____

1.8 CROSS OUT THE INCORRECT WORDS IN EACH SENTENCE, THEN SAY THE SENTENCES OUT LOUD

> I'm sorry, how **do you say** / ~~are you saying~~ your name again?

1 Hello Frank. **Are you enjoying** / **do you enjoy** the conference?

2 Wilfred, I'd like you to **meet** / **be meeting** Roger, our new press officer.

3 Serena, it's really great to **see** / **seeing** you again after so long.

4 I usually enjoy workshops, but I am not **find** / **finding** this one interesting.

---

01 ✓ CHECKLIST

⚙ Present simple and continuous ☐   **Aa** Etiquette for introductions ☐   🧩 Introducing yourself and others ☐

02 Getting to know colleagues

Talking about your past work experience is a good way to get to know your colleagues. Past simple and past continuous tenses are often used to do this.

⚙ **New language** Past simple and past continuous
Aa Vocabulary Sharing past experiences
🧩 **New skill** Talking about past experiences

2.1 KEY LANGUAGE THE PAST SIMPLE AND THE PAST CONTINUOUS

Use the past simple to talk about a single, completed action in the past, past habits, or a state that was true for a time in the past.

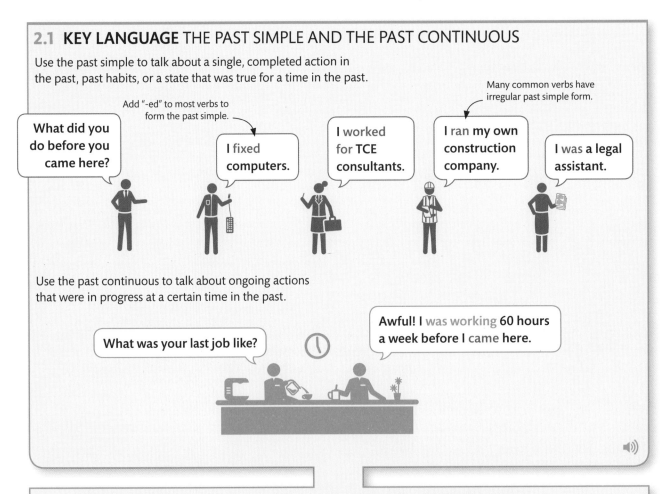

Add "-ed" to most verbs to form the past simple.

Many common verbs have irregular past simple form.

What did you do before you came here?

I fixed computers.

I worked for TCE consultants.

I ran my own construction company.

I was a legal assistant.

Use the past continuous to talk about ongoing actions that were in progress at a certain time in the past.

What was your last job like?

Awful! I was working 60 hours a week before I came here.

2.2 HOW TO FORM THE PAST SIMPLE AND THE PAST CONTINUOUS

The past simple is usually formed by adding "-ed" to the base form of the verb. The past continuous is formed by adding "was" or "were" in front of the verb, and "-ing" to the end of the verb.

SUBJECT	PAST CONTINUOUS	REST OF CLAUSE	PAST SIMPLE
I	was working	60 hours a week	before I came here.

2.3 CROSS OUT THE INCORRECT WORDS IN EACH SENTENCE

> I **started** / ~~was starting~~ my own printing company more than 10 years ago.

❶ They **began** / were beginning to sell more when the shop suddenly closed last year.

❷ I **lost** / was losing my job when the factory closed last December.

❸ I was delighted when I **got** / was getting promoted to senior manager in 2015.

❹ We moved here when my wife was finding / **found** a new job two years ago.

❺ I was training / **trained** to be a chef when I was given this award.

❻ When I worked 90 hours a week, I **felt** / was feeling exhausted all the time.

❼ When I was a photographer, I was meeting / **met** a lot of famous people through my work.

2.4 **KEY LANGUAGE** THE PAST TENSE FOR POLITENESS

You may hear people ask questions about a present situation in the past tense. This makes the question more polite.

"Do" becomes "Did" to make the question in past tense.

> Did **you want a tour of the office?**

The past tense is also sometimes used to make a polite request.

> I **wanted to ask about the company's history.**

2.5 MARK THE SENTENCES THAT ARE CORRECT

> Did you want some more coffee? ✓
> Do you wanting some more coffee? ☐

❶ I was to look for another job. ☐
I was looking for another job. ☐

❷ I was wondering if you could help. ☐
I was wondered if you could help. ☐

❸ Were you working as a waiter? ☐
Were you work as a waiter? ☐

❹ They weren't employing young people. ☐
They not employing young people. ☐

❺ I didn't enjoy my last job. ☐
I didn't enjoying my last job. ☐

❻ Did you work in a hotel? ☐
Did you working in a hotel? ☐

2.6 KEY LANGUAGE THE PRESENT PERFECT SIMPLE

The present perfect simple is used to talk about events in the recent past that still have an effect on the present moment.

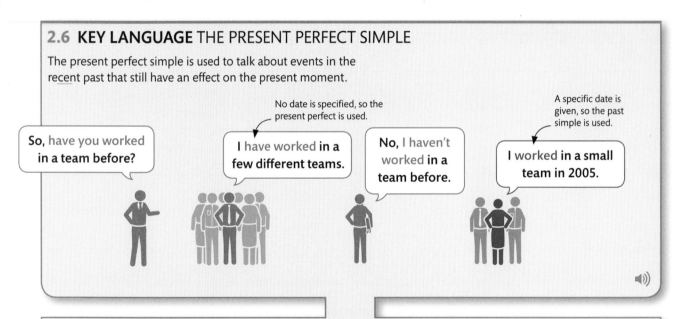

So, have you worked in a team before?

No date is specified, so the present perfect is used.

I have worked in a few different teams.

No, I haven't worked in a team before.

A specific date is given, so the past simple is used.

I worked in a small team in 2005.

2.7 HOW TO FORM THE PRESENT PERFECT SIMPLE

The present perfect simple is formed with "have" and a past participle.

SUBJECT	"HAVE / HAS" + PAST PARTICIPLE	REST OF SENTENCE
I	have worked	in a few teams.

2.8 FILL IN THE GAPS BY PUTTING THE VERBS IN THE PRESENT PERFECT SIMPLE

Susan ___has worked___ (work) here since she graduated from college five years ago.

❶ He _____ (take) 15 days off sick this year already and it is only May!

❷ Julia has a lot of experience. She _____ (manage) this department for years.

❸ They _____ (employ) more than 300 people over the years.

❹ John _____ (train) lots of young employees across a few different teams.

❺ I'm so happy! I _____ (finish) my apprenticeship at last.

❻ My manager _____ (approve) my vacation days. I'm going to Italy in July.

2.9 LISTEN TO THE AUDIO AND ANSWER THE QUESTIONS

Two colleagues are discussing their past experience.

This is Suzi's first day at the company.
True ☐   False ☐   Not given ✓

❶ Suzi's previous company was smaller.
True ☐   False ☐   Not given ☐

❷ Suzi has always worked in HR.
True ☐   False ☐   Not given ☐

❸ Jack has worked for CIE for six years.
True ☐   False ☐   Not given ☐

❹ Jack has never worked for another company.
True ☐   False ☐   Not given ☐

❺ Jack and Suzi always work the same days.
True ☐   False ☐   Not given ☐

2.10 CROSS OUT THE INCORRECT WORDS IN EACH SENTENCE, THEN SAY THE SENTENCES OUT LOUD

I ~~worked~~ / ~~was working~~ / have worked in marketing since 1995.

❶ I drove / was driving / have driven taxis when I saw this job advertised.

❷ I managed / was managing / have managed accounts for this company for seven years.

❸ I bought / was buying / have bought my first business in 2009.

❹ I was studying in college when I saw / was seeing / have seen this job.

❺ They invested / were investing / have invested in this company since 2010.

❻ In 2014, I sold / was selling / has sold the company to an investor.

---

02 ✓ **CHECKLIST**

⚙ Past simple and past continuous ☐   **Aa** Sharing past experiences ☐   Talking about past experiences ☐

3.1 DEPARTMENTS

Administration

[deals with organization and internal and external communication]

Production

[ensures all manufacturing stages run smoothly]

Research and Development (R&D)

[deals with researching and developing future products for a company]

Purchasing

[deals with buying goods and raw materials]

Human Resources (HR)

[deals with employee relations and matters such as hiring staff]

Sales

[deals with selling a finished product to outside markets]

Accounts / Finance

[deals with money matters, from paying bills to projecting sales]

Facilities / Office Services

[ensures the smooth day-to-day running of the practical aspects of a company]

Marketing

[deals with promoting products]

Legal

[ensures that all contracts and company activities are legal]

Public Relations (PR)

[deals with maintaining a positive public image for a company]

Information Technology (IT)

[ensures that all technological systems are working and maintained]

3.2 ROLES

employer

Chief Executive
Officer (CEO)

manager

employee

Chief Financial Officer
(CFO)

assistant

3.3 DESCRIBING ROLES

We all work for a large department store.

to work for
[to be employed by a company]

He looks after our salaries and wages.

to look after
[to ensure something runs smoothly]

I work in event management.

to work in
[to be employed in a department or area of an industry]

They are responsible for office maintenance.

to be responsible for
[to have the duty of ensuring something is done effectively]

She works as a fashion designer.

to work as
[to have a particular job or role]

I'm in charge of administration.

to be in charge of
[to have control and authority over something]

04 Talking about changes

There are many ways to talk about changes at work in the past and present. Many of the phrases include "used to," which can have several different meanings.

🔧 **New language** "Used to," "be / get used to"
Aa Vocabulary Small talk
🧩 **New skill** Talking about changes at work

4.1 KEY LANGUAGE "USED TO," "GET USED TO," AND "BE USED TO"

"Used" with an infinitive describes a regular habit or state in the past.

"To eat" is the infinitive form of the verb.

Staff used to eat **lunch at their desks.**

"Get used to" describes the process of becoming familiar with something.

"Get used to" can be followed by a noun or gerund.

It took a while to get used to **the commute.
commuting.**

"Be used to" describes being familiar with something.

"Be used to" can be followed by a noun or gerund.

Nowadays I am used to **waking up early.
early mornings.**

4.2 FURTHER EXAMPLES "USED TO," "GET USED TO," AND "BE USED TO"

In questions and negatives, there is no "d" after "use."

Did you use to **do everything by hand in the factory?**

We didn't use to **have so much construction in the area.**

I don't know that I will ever get used to these uniforms!

After working here for a decade, we are used to **the noise.**

4.3 MARK THE SENTENCES THAT ARE CORRECT

He is used to working from home. ✓
He is use to working from home. ☐

1. I use to travel to work by car. ☐
   I used to travel to work by car. ☐

2. She's used to giving big presentations. ☐
   She's used to give big presentations. ☐

3. I'll get used to my new job eventually. ☐
   I get used my new job eventually. ☐

4. We didn't used to get paid a bonus. ☐
   We didn't use to get paid a bonus. ☐

5. Did he use to work in marketing? ☐
   Did he used to work in marketing? ☐

🔊

4.4 LISTEN TO THE AUDIO, THEN NUMBER THE PICTURES IN THE ORDER THEY ARE DESCRIBED

A ☐

B 1

C ☐

D ☐

4.5 REWRITE THE SENTENCES, PUTTING THE WORDS IN THE CORRECT ORDER

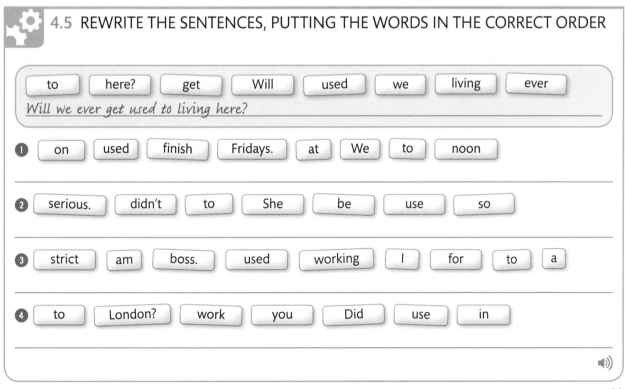

| to | here? | get | Will | used | we | living | ever |

Will we ever get used to living here?

1. | on | used | finish | Fridays. | at | We | to | noon |
_____

2. | serious. | didn't | to | She | be | use | so |
_____

3. | strict | am | boss. | used | working | I | for | to | a |
_____

4. | to | London? | work | you | Did | use | in |
_____

🔊

23

4.6 MATCH THE PAIRS OF PHRASES THAT MEAN THE SAME THING

I was a bank employee in the past. → I used to work in a bank.

Did he use to work in a bank?

1 I began working long days early in my career.

2 He is a qualified lawyer now.

3 I don't usually work short days.

4 Your working day was shorter in the past.

5 Has he worked in a bank before?

You didn't use to work such long hours.

I am used to working long hours.

He didn't use to have a law degree.

I got used to long hours in my first job.

4.7 READ THE ARTICLE AND ANSWER THE QUESTIONS

Weather is a common topic for small talk.
True ✓ **False** ☐ **Not given** ☐

1 Being good at small talk can give you an advantage in your job.
True ☐ **False** ☐ **Not given** ☐

2 Sports are the most common topic for small talk.
True ☐ **False** ☐ **Not given** ☐

3 People who are good at small talk are generally disliked.
True ☐ **False** ☐ **Not given** ☐

4 When talking to a colleague, don't look at their face.
True ☐ **False** ☐ **Not given** ☐

5 Not every topic is suitable for small talk.
True ☐ **False** ☐ **Not given** ☐

It's good to talk

Small talk—chatting about trivial topics such as the weather

"Morning, Sammy. Did you see the game last night?" This kind of small talk happens in every office around the world, every day. People who make an effort to talk to others are more well-liked by their colleagues. When you make small talk, you make the other person feel more relaxed, and form a connection with that person. People who are good at small talk tend to be quick thinkers, and businesses like employees who can think on their feet. So what are the key skills you need to master to be good at small talk? Make eye contact with the other person, and listen. Be interested in what they have to say. Stick to topics such as hobbies, books, films, and the weather. And avoid uncomfortable topics such as politics, religion, and money.

24

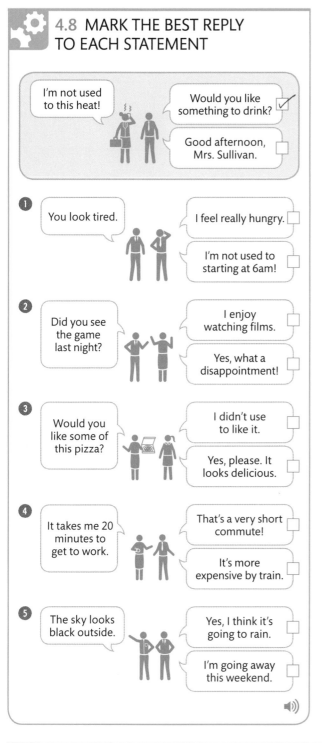

4.8 MARK THE BEST REPLY TO EACH STATEMENT

I'm not used to this heat!

Would you like something to drink? ✓

Good afternoon, Mrs. Sullivan. ☐

1 You look tired.

I feel really hungry. ☐

I'm not used to starting at 6am! ☐

2 Did you see the game last night?

I enjoy watching films. ☐

Yes, what a disappointment! ☐

3 Would you like some of this pizza?

I didn't use to like it. ☐

Yes, please. It looks delicious. ☐

4 It takes me 20 minutes to get to work.

That's a very short commute! ☐

It's more expensive by train. ☐

5 The sky looks black outside.

Yes, I think it's going to rain. ☐

I'm going away this weekend. ☐

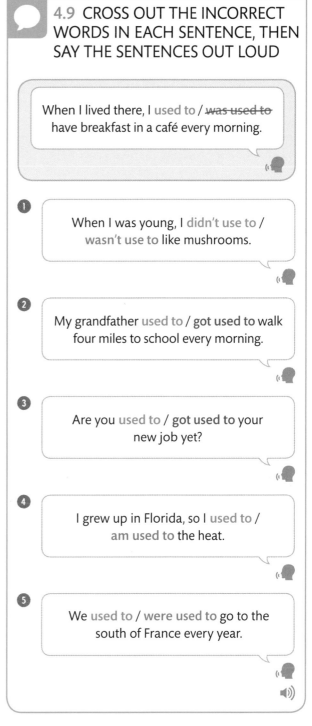

4.9 CROSS OUT THE INCORRECT WORDS IN EACH SENTENCE, THEN SAY THE SENTENCES OUT LOUD

When I lived there, I used to / ~~was used to~~ have breakfast in a café every morning.

1 When I was young, I didn't use to / wasn't use to like mushrooms.

2 My grandfather used to / got used to walk four miles to school every morning.

3 Are you used to / got used to your new job yet?

4 I grew up in Florida, so I used to / am used to the heat.

5 We used to / were used to go to the south of France every year.

04 ✅ **CHECKLIST**		
⚙ "Used to," "be / get used to" ☐	**Aa** Small talk ☐	🧩 Talking about changes at work ☐

25

05 Delegating tasks

When things get busy, you may want to delegate tasks to colleagues. To do this, different modal verbs are used in English to show the level of obligation.

 **New language** Modal verbs for obligation
Aa Vocabulary Delegation and politeness
New skill Delegating tasks to colleagues

5.1 KEY LANGUAGE MODAL VERBS FOR OBLIGATION

Certain modal verbs can be used to say that someone needs to do something.

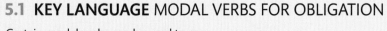

I { **have to** / **have got to** / **need to** } **leave this with you.**

"Need" acts like a modal verb here, expressing strong obligation.

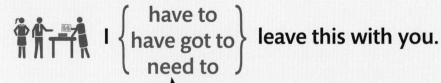

You don't have to deal with this today.

"Don't have to" means that there is no obligation to do something.

You must complete this project by Monday.

"Must" is a direct, and sometimes impolite, way to say something needs to be done.

You must not go into the testing area.

"Must not" means that something is prohibited.

5.2 HOW TO FORM MODAL VERBS FOR OBLIGATION

"Must" does not change with the subject, but "have to" becomes "has to" in the third person singular. Both are followed by the base form of the main verb.

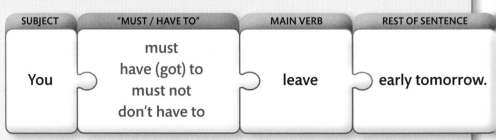

SUBJECT	"MUST / HAVE TO"	MAIN VERB	REST OF SENTENCE
You	must / have (got) to / must not / don't have to	leave	early tomorrow.

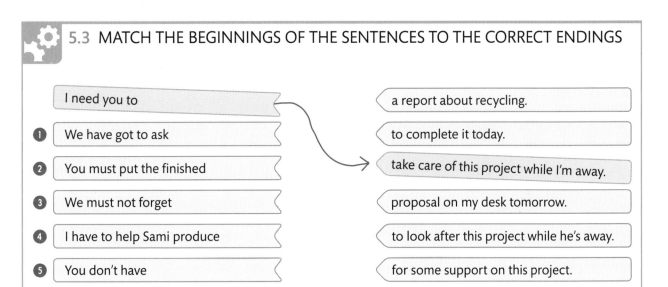

5.3 MATCH THE BEGINNINGS OF THE SENTENCES TO THE CORRECT ENDINGS

I need you to	a report about recycling.
❶ We have got to ask	to complete it today.
❷ You must put the finished	take care of this project while I'm away.
❸ We must not forget	proposal on my desk tomorrow.
❹ I have to help Sami produce	to look after this project while he's away.
❺ You don't have	for some support on this project.

I need you to → take care of this project while I'm away.

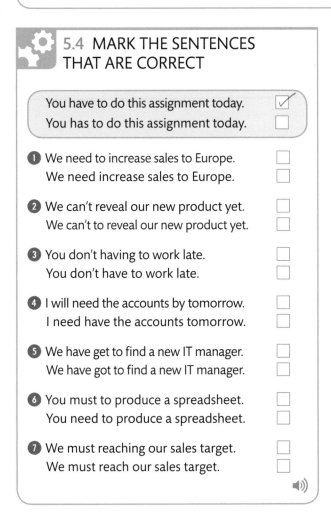

5.4 MARK THE SENTENCES THAT ARE CORRECT

You have to do this assignment today. ☑
You has to do this assignment today. ☐

❶ We need to increase sales to Europe. ☐
We need increase sales to Europe. ☐

❷ We can't reveal our new product yet. ☐
We can't to reveal our new product yet. ☐

❸ You don't having to work late. ☐
You don't have to work late. ☐

❹ I will need the accounts by tomorrow. ☐
I need have the accounts tomorrow. ☐

❺ We have get to find a new IT manager. ☐
We have got to find a new IT manager. ☐

❻ You must to produce a spreadsheet. ☐
You need to produce a spreadsheet. ☐

❼ We must reaching our sales target. ☐
We must reach our sales target. ☐

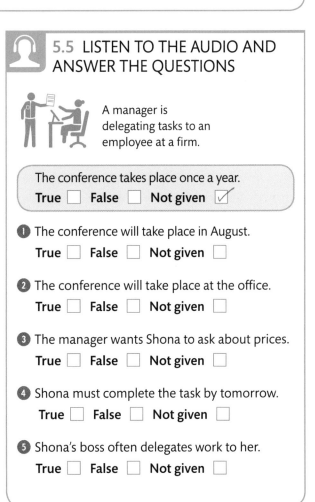

5.5 LISTEN TO THE AUDIO AND ANSWER THE QUESTIONS

A manager is delegating tasks to an employee at a firm.

The conference takes place once a year.
True ☐ **False** ☐ **Not given** ☑

❶ The conference will take place in August.
True ☐ **False** ☐ **Not given** ☐

❷ The conference will take place at the office.
True ☐ **False** ☐ **Not given** ☐

❸ The manager wants Shona to ask about prices.
True ☐ **False** ☐ **Not given** ☐

❹ Shona must complete the task by tomorrow.
True ☐ **False** ☐ **Not given** ☐

❺ Shona's boss often delegates work to her.
True ☐ **False** ☐ **Not given** ☐

5.6 KEY LANGUAGE POLITENESS

To maintain a friendly, polite atmosphere, you can use "we" instead of "you" to express obligation.

We have to finish this project soon

Other modal verbs can also be used in business to delegate tasks politely.

Could
Would } you look after this for me?

"Would" is more formal and is rarely used.

5.7 REWRITE THE SENTENCES, PUTTING THE WORDS IN THE CORRECT ORDER

| you | print | copy? | a | Could | me |

Could you print me a copy?

1 | you | answer | my | Could | phone? |

2 | you | Would | call | the | supplier? |

3 | We | to | have | today. | finish |

4 | you | Would | a | book | meeting? |

5 | send | this | Could | you | today? |

5.8 CROSS OUT THE INCORRECT WORDS IN EACH SENTENCE, THEN SAY THE SENTENCES OUT LOUD

Don't worry! You **don't have to** / ~~must not~~ deal with this right now.

1 Could / Have you deliver this letter for me, please?

2 Must / Would you show the new employee around the office?

3 Jess, I have got / need to leave early today. Could you let Philippe know?

5.9 READ THE ARTICLE AND ANSWER THE QUESTIONS

> Team leaders should do everyday tasks.
> **True** ☐ **False** ☐ **Not given** ☑

1 A routine task is answering customer enquiries.
True ☐ **False** ☐ **Not given** ☐

2 People who don't delegate often feel stressed.
True ☐ **False** ☐ **Not given** ☐

3 A team leader has to avoid doing everyday tasks.
True ☐ **False** ☐ **Not given** ☐

4 Trust in managers is falling in most companies.
True ☐ **False** ☐ **Not given** ☐

5 Team leaders should trust their staff.
True ☐ **False** ☐ **Not given** ☐

BUSINESS WEEKLY

Sharing the load

Relieve stress by learning to delegate better

Team leaders must think about goals and how to achieve them. This takes time. You won't have this thinking time if you're busy doing routine tasks and you will feel stressed. You have to let your team members handle the everyday tasks. Show your team members you trust them. Ask them if they could show you a plan of how they can manage their work in their own way. This way you will build a better working relationship.

---

05 ✓ CHECKLIST

⚙ Modal verbs for obligation ☐   **Aa** Delegation and politeness ☐   🧩 Delegating tasks to colleagues ☐

🔄 REVIEW THE ENGLISH YOU HAVE LEARNED IN UNITS 1–5

NEW LANGUAGE	SAMPLE SENTENCE	☑	UNIT
INTRODUCING YOURSELF AND OTHERS	You must be Eric from the UK. Tony, this is Hayao from our Japanese office.	☐	1.1
THE PAST SIMPLE AND THE PAST CONTINUOUS FOR PAST EXPERIENCES	I was working 60 hours per week when I came here.	☐	2.1
THE PAST TENSE FOR POLITENESS	Did you want a tour of the office?	☐	2.4
TALKING ABOUT THE RECENT PAST WITH THE PRESENT PERFECT SIMPLE	I have worked in a few different teams.	☐	2.6
TALKING ABOUT CHANGES WITH "USED TO" AND "BE / GET USED TO"	Staff used to eat lunch at their desks. It took a while to get used to the commute.	☐	4.1
DELEGATING TASKS WITH MODALS	I have to leave this with you. Could you look after this for me?	☐	5.1, 5.6

6.1 MONEY AND FINANCE

The company's income fell last year.

income
[money coming into a business]

The initial expenditure on technology was huge, but now we can work faster.

expenditure / outlay
[an amount of money spent]

We have a large budget for this movie, so the effects will be amazing.

a budget
[the amount of money that is available to spend on something]

We must do all we can to avoid getting into debt.

to get into debt
[to get into a situation where you owe people money]

The bank charges for overdrafts now.

an overdraft
[extra money the bank allows you to spend]

The profit margin on these T-shirts is huge!

a profit margin
[the difference between the cost of making or buying something and what it's sold for]

We need to sell two cars to break even.

to break even
[to earn just enough to cover the costs of producing a product]

We haven't sold enough pineapples. We've made a loss.

to make a loss
[to lose money by spending more than you earn]

We need to make sure the accounts are always up to date.

accounts
[records of money paid into and out of a business]

High overheads make this business difficult to run.

overheads
[the regular costs of running a business, such as wages]

I'm selling these earrings at cost to attract customers.

cost (US) / cost price (UK)
[a sales price that covers the costs of producing an item without making a profit]

Our clients need to pay now or we will have a cash flow problem.

cash flow
[the rate at which money comes into and goes out of a business]

The prices peaked in June, but they're down now.

to peak
[to reach the highest point]

It's always hard to see a company go out of business.

to go out of business
[to no longer be able to exist as a business]

When the CEO left, the company's value dropped.

to drop
[to fall, especially in worth or value]

We need to undercut our competitors or we will lose customers.

to undercut competitors
[to charge less than others who sell the same goods or services as you]

Changes in the exchange rate make the market uncertain.

the exchange rate
[the amount of one currency that you get when you change it for another]

Our sales figures have improved consistently each year.

sales figures
[the amount or value of total sales over a particular period]

Thankfully, there was an upturn in the market.

an upturn in the market
[a change to more positive business conditions]

Everyone suffered because of the economic downturn last year.

an economic downturn
[a major decline in economic activity]

07 Writing a report

When writing a report, you may need to use different past tenses to show sequences of events. You may also need to use more formal phrasing.

⚙ **New language** Past perfect and past simple
Aa Vocabulary Formal business English
🧩 **New skill** Writing reports

7.1 KEY LANGUAGE PAST PERFECT AND PAST SIMPLE

English uses the past perfect and the past simple together to describe past events that occurred at different times. The past simple describes the event that is closest to the time of speaking.

PAST PERFECT PAST SIMPLE

Sales of our cleaning products had fallen, so we hired a new marketing team.

TWO MONTHS AGO   ONE MONTH AGO

7.2 FURTHER EXAMPLES PAST PERFECT AND PAST SIMPLE

Add "not" or its short form after "had" to form negatives.

Many of our customers hadn't tried online shopping before we launched our delivery service.

Invert "had" and the subject to form questions.

Had you prepared for that presentation? It didn't go very well.

7.3 HOW TO FORM THE PAST PERFECT

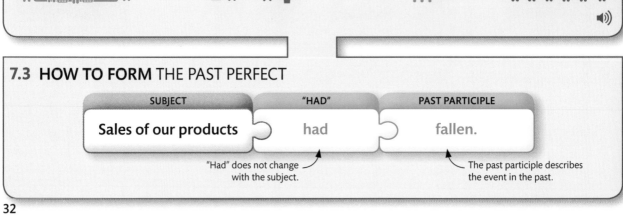

SUBJECT	"HAD"	PAST PARTICIPLE
Sales of our products	had	fallen.

"Had" does not change with the subject.

The past participle describes the event in the past.

7.4 FILL IN THE GAPS BY PUTTING THE VERBS IN THE PAST PERFECT OR PAST SIMPLE

The number of complaints _had risen_ (rise), so we _sent_ (send) our staff for training.

1. We _____ (change) our logo because a lot of people _____ (complain) about it.

2. Some of our goods _____ (arrive) broken, so we _____ (ask) for a refund.

3. There _____ (be) problems in the warehouse because our manager _____ (resign).

4. Sales of umbrellas _____ (be) poor because we _____ (have) a dry summer.

5. Our clients _____ (not be) happy because we _____ (miss) our deadline.

6. Yasmin's presentation _____ (go) very well, so I _____ (give) her a promotion.

7. Our sales _____ (increase) because we _____ (launch) a new product range.

◀))

7.5 READ THE REPORT AND MARK THE CORRECT SUMMARY

1. The trial had mostly negative results and the report recommends returning to telephone operators only. ☐

2. The trial had both positive and negative results and the report recommends maintaining both systems. ☐

3. The trial had mostly positive results and the report recommends keeping the trial online messaging only. ☐

Replacement of Telephone Operators with Online Messaging

Guil Motors replaced all its telephone operators with online messaging for a trial period.

Benefits:
• Each operator can deal with more than one client
• A written record is kept of each dialogue

Negative effects:
• Significant drop in number of inquiries
• Customer dissatisfaction

Recommendations:
• Offer both phone and online messaging services
• Create positive promotion for online messaging

7.6 KEY LANGUAGE PROJECT REPORTS

Here are some examples of formal language typically found in project reports.

Formal alternative to "This report shows."

The following report presents the results of a client satisfaction survey.

Use the infinitive with "to" to talk about purpose.

The purpose of this report is to review our marketing expenditure.

Formal reports often use the passive voice.

As can be seen in the table, we spent very little on social media marketing.

Formal alternative to "said."

Our clients stated that they had been disappointed with the sales figures.

Formal alternative to "first."

Based on this initial research, we should increase our marketing budget.

Formal alternative to "main."

My principal recommendation is to create and launch a new campaign.

 ## 7.7 REWRITE THE SENTENCES, CORRECTING THE ERRORS

Many of our clients was interviewed for this report.
Many of our clients were interviewed for this report.

❶ The purpose of this report is review our sales figures for the last quarter.

_____

❷ Our principle recommendation is to complete the sale of the downtown store.

_____

❸ The follow report presents the results of extensive customer satisfaction research.

_____

❹ Our main client state that the recent changes were beneficial for his business.

_____

7.8 MATCH THE BEGINNINGS OF THE SENTENCES TO THE CORRECT ENDINGS

The following report presents → our staffing plans for the coming year.

that there were a number of problems.

1. As can be seen in the table,

to present the findings of our survey.

2. It is clear from the research

our staffing plans for the coming year.

3. A number of focus groups

the figures for this period were excellent.

4. The purpose of this report is

were consulted for this report.

7.9 FILL IN THE GAPS USING THE WORDS IN THE PANEL

Our clients _____ stated _____ that they had been disappointed with our products.

1. The focus group clients had all _____ both the original and new products.

2. The following chart _____ the sales figures for the two periods.

3. We _____ the customers who had complained why they didn't like the change.

4. The _____ of this report is to present the results of our online trial.

5. We started this online trial after our store costs had _____ by 10 percent.

| compares | ~~stated~~ | asked | risen | used | purpose |

🔧 Past perfect and past simple ☐   **Aa** Formal business English ☐   🧩 Writing reports ☐

08

Making apologies

The present perfect continuous describes ongoing situations in the past that may affect the present. It can be used in apologies and to give reasons for problems.

New language Present perfect continuous
Aa Vocabulary Apologies
New skill Apologizing on the telephone

8.1 KEY LANGUAGE TELEPHONE APOLOGIES

English uses a variety of phrases for making apologies, offering to investigate a problem, and offering explanations and solutions.

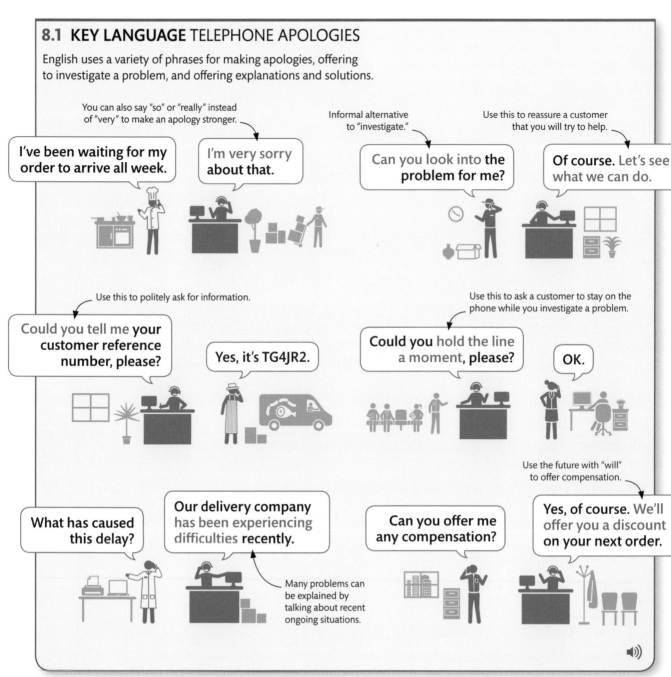

You can also say "so" or "really" instead of "very" to make an apology stronger.

I've been waiting for my order to arrive all week.

I'm very sorry about that.

Informal alternative to "investigate."

Can you look into the problem for me?

Use this to reassure a customer that you will try to help.

Of course. Let's see what we can do.

Use this to politely ask for information.

Could you tell me your customer reference number, please?

Yes, it's TG4JR2.

Use this to ask a customer to stay on the phone while you investigate a problem.

Could you hold the line a moment, please?

OK.

What has caused this delay?

Our delivery company has been experiencing difficulties recently.

Many problems can be explained by talking about recent ongoing situations.

Can you offer me any compensation?

Use the future with "will" to offer compensation.

Yes, of course. We'll offer you a discount on your next order.

Aa 8.2 MATCH THE SENTENCES TO THE CORRECT RESPONSES

Can you look into the problem for me?

1 Could I have a refund?

2 Could you tell me your order number?

3 Could you hold the line a moment, please?

4 Why isn't my order here yet?

5 My order arrived dirty and broken.

6 Will you send me a replacement?

Yes, we'll send you a new one tomorrow.

Our courier has been having difficulties.

Of course. Let's see what we can do.

I'm very sorry to hear that, Mrs. Singh.

Yes, we'll give you a full refund.

OK. No problem.

Yes, it's AMLGW14.

8.3 LISTEN TO THE AUDIO, THEN NUMBER THE PHRASES IN THE ORDER YOU HEAR THEM

Ethan takes a phone call from a customer who wants to complain about an order she has placed.

A Let's see what I can do. ☐

B I'm really sorry to hear that. ☐ 1

C We'll offer a discount on your next order. ☐

D The driver has been stuck in traffic. ☐

E Could you tell me your order number? ☐

F Could you hold the line a moment, please? ☐

8.4 CROSS OUT THE INCORRECT WORD IN EACH SENTENCE, THEN SAY THE SENTENCES OUT LOUD

I'm sorry / ~~much~~ about the delay.

1 We'll see / look into the problem for you.

2 We'll give / giving you a discount voucher.

3 Could you hold the phone / line a moment?

4 Let's see what / when we can do.

8.5 KEY LANGUAGE THE PRESENT PERFECT CONTINUOUS

The present perfect continuous describes an ongoing situation in the past that often affects the present moment. You can use it to offer explanations for problems.

Our delivery company has been experiencing **difficulties recently.**

PRESENT PERFECT CONTINUOUS

The situation usually affects the present moment or recent past.

8.6 FURTHER EXAMPLES THE PRESENT PERFECT CONTINUOUS

We haven't been getting **good feedback lately.**

Add "not" or its short form after "have" or "has" to form the negative.

I'm really sorry for the delay. Have you been waiting **all morning?**

In questions, the subject sits between "have" or "has" and "been."

8.7 HOW TO FORM THE PRESENT PERFECT CONTINUOUS

SUBJECT	"HAS / HAVE"	BEEN	VERB + "-ING"	REST OF SENTENCE
Our delivery company	has	been	experiencing	difficulties.

Use "has" or "have," depending on the subject.

"Been" stays the same for all subjects.

Add "-ing" to the main verb.

8.8 FILL IN THE GAPS BY PUTTING THE VERBS IN THE PRESENT PERFECT CONTINUOUS

Our customers ___have been complaining___ (complain) about our poor service recently.

1. The customers _____ (wait) for us to contact them.

2. Our engineers _____ (work) on the line for two days.

3. What _____ you _____ (do) to solve the problem?

4. I _____ (watch) your program and I want to complain.

5. We _____ (repair) the broken cables this morning.

6. They _____ (update) my software and now it doesn't work.

◀))

8.9 READ THE EMAIL AND ANSWER THE QUESTIONS

The complaint is about train delays.
True ✓   **False** ☐   **Not given** ☐

1. RailKo says they are sorry about the delay.
True ☐   **False** ☐   **Not given** ☐

2. RailKo says the thieves were found.
True ☐   **False** ☐   **Not given** ☐

3. The problem was unexpected for RailKo.
True ☐   **False** ☐   **Not given** ☐

4. RailKo offers Ms. Pérez a total refund.
True ☐   **False** ☐   **Not given** ☐

5. RailKo will keep passengers up to date with changes.
True ☐   **False** ☐   **Not given** ☐

✉ ∨ ✕

To: Mariana Pérez

Subject: Severe train delay

Dear Ms. Pérez,
Thank you for your email regarding the delay to your trip on July 11th. I've been investigating the problem and see that your train was, indeed, 70 minutes late. We apologize for the inconvenience this caused. We've been upgrading that line for several weeks and unfortunately that morning thieves stole a lot of machinery and it was not safe for trains to travel at their usual speed. As you can imagine, RailKo was unable to predict this event. By way of an apology, however, we'd like to offer you a refund of 50% of the value of your ticket. I've attached the voucher to this email.

Yours sincerely,
Joshua Hawkins

↩ ↩↩   📎 🗑

08 ✓ CHECKLIST

⚙ Present perfect continuous ☐   **Aa** Apologies ☐   🧩 Apologizing on the telephone ☐

Vocabulary

9.1 COMMUNICATION TECHNOLOGY

I can access my work emails from my home computer.

to access
[to enter or connect to something]

I appear to have lost access to the network again!

a network
[a system of interconnected technology]

As a company we always keep our hardware and apps up to date.

up to date
[current and modern]

We have an automated voicemail system.

automated
[computerized; not operated by a human]

My phone is connected to the network so I can receive emails any time.

connected to
[in communication with]

Most people in the office carry a mobile device with them.

a mobile device
[a small computing device, such as a smartphone or tablet, that is easily carried]

For most of the day I have to work online to access the internet and emails.

to work online
[to work with an internet connection]

I work offline when commuting to work because there is no internet on the train.

to work offline
[to work without an internet connection]

If you download the app, you'll get updates about new products.

to download an app
[to get an application from the internet onto a device or computer]

I automatically back up my documents every 15 minutes.

to back up
[to save an extra copy of a document in case the original is lost]

This new program is very user-friendly.

user-friendly
[easy for the operator to use]

I must have the wrong address. My email has bounced.

an email has bounced
[an email has been automatically returned without reaching the intended recipient]

Our new website works on computers and mobile devices.

a website
[a collection of linked pages accessed through the internet]

I often use social media to look for job vacancies.

social media
[internet-based tools for communicating with friends and communities]

I'm sorry, I can't hear you properly. You're breaking up.

breaking up
[losing a phone or internet connection]

Can you arrange a videoconference with the clients in Sydney?

a videoconference
[a conference by phone or via the internet in which people can see and talk to each other]

Let's arrange a conference call so we can all catch up.

a conference call
[a group conversation held by phone]

Please could you charge the tablet before the meeting?

to charge
[to connect a mobile device to electricity to give it more power]

Our company always uses the latest software.

software
[computer programs]

When you create your account, you get a username and password.

a username and password
[a name and code used to access an account on a computing device]

10 Making plans by email

English uses a variety of phrases to make and check plans with co-workers by email. It is important to ensure that even informal messages are polite.

⚙️ **New language** Email language
Aa Vocabulary Meetings and workshops
🧩 **New skill** Making plans

10.1 KEY LANGUAGE EMAILS TO CO-WORKERS

In business emails, it is important to use polite and clear language to exchange information with co-workers. Emails to co-workers are often less formal than emails to clients or senior personnel.

TIP
Keep your style consistent. For example, if you add a comma after your greeting, remember to add one after your sign-off, too.

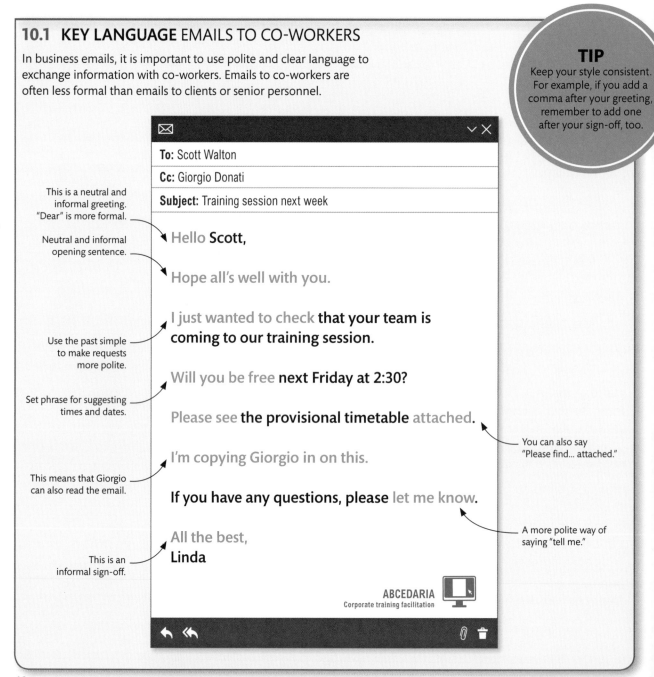

To: Scott Walton
Cc: Giorgio Donati
Subject: Training session next week

Hello **Scott,**

Hope all's well with you.

I just wanted to check **that your team is coming to our training session.**

Will you be free **next Friday at 2:30?**

Please see **the provisional timetable** attached.

I'm copying Giorgio in on this.

If you have any questions, please let me know.

All the best,
Linda

ABCEDARIA
Corporate training facilitation

- This is a neutral and informal greeting. "Dear" is more formal.
- Neutral and informal opening sentence.
- Use the past simple to make requests more polite.
- Set phrase for suggesting times and dates.
- This means that Giorgio can also read the email.
- This is an informal sign-off.
- You can also say "Please find... attached."
- A more polite way of saying "tell me."

10.2 READ THE EMAIL AND MARK THE CORRECT SUMMARY

1. Mira is emailing Catherine to check that she is coming to a sales presentation in Room A. Pauline is also invited to the presentation. ☐

2. Mira wants to meet next Friday to discuss arrangements for the sales presentation. She has asked Pauline to send her the agenda. ☐

3. Mira is inviting Catherine to a meeting to discuss arrangements for the sales presentation. She has sent Catherine and Pauline the timetable and agenda. ☐

4. Mira is emailing to check that Pauline is coming to the sales presentation. Catherine has sent the timetable and agenda. ☐

To: Catherine Quint

Subject: Sales presentation

Hi Catherine,

Hope all's well with you. I just wanted to check that you got my earlier email about our sales presentation next Friday. Pauline and I are meeting this morning to discuss arrangements. Will you be free to come and join us in Room A at 11:30?

Please find the attached timetable and agenda for the presentation. I've copied Pauline in on this message. If you have any ideas or want to ask any questions, please let me know.

All the best,
Mira

Copy&Print Sprint

10.3 FILL IN THE GAPS USING THE WORDS IN THE PANEL

Please see the timetable for tomorrow's training course ___attached___ .

1. I just wanted to _____ that you will be able to make it to the meeting.

2. Don't worry if you have any questions. Just let me _____ .

3. I'm _____ Maxine in on this as she may have some more information.

4. How _____ coming to the restaurant with us this evening?

5. I was _____ if you and Ana could come to the meeting tomorrow.

6. Give me a call if you can't _____ the presentation at 10 o'clock.

know
copying
attached
wondering
check
about
make

---

11 Keeping clients informed

Use the present continuous to inform clients about current situations and future arrangements. Continuous tenses can also soften questions and requests.

⚙ **New language** Continuous tenses
Aa Vocabulary Arrangements and schedules
🧩 **New skill** Keeping clients informed

11.1 KEY LANGUAGE THE PRESENT CONTINUOUS

English uses the present continuous to describe what's happening right now.

Use "still" to emphasize that a situation is ongoing.

We are aiming to give you a full progress report.

We are still waiting for a part from our supplier.

English also uses the present continuous to talk about arrangements for a fixed time in the future.

Use the present continuous with a future time marker to talk about future arrangements.

We are having a meeting with the IT department later today.

Malik is talking to HR next week to discuss the noise issues.

🔊

11.2 LISTEN TO THE AUDIO AND MARK WHETHER THE ACTIVITY IN EACH PICTURE TAKES PLACE IN THE PRESENT OR THE FUTURE

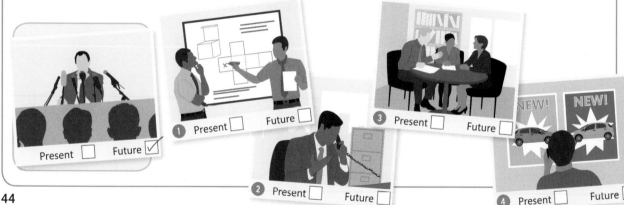

Present ☐ Future ✓

① Present ☐ Future ☐

② Present ☐ Future ☐

③ Present ☐ Future ☐

④ Present ☐ Future ☐

11.3 READ THE EMAIL AND WRITE ANSWERS TO THE QUESTIONS AS FULL SENTENCES

To: Yasmin Hendricks

Subject: Delay with order TY309

Dear Ms. Hendricks,

I'm sorry to inform you that our delivery van was involved in an accident yesterday. I've obtained a list of affected customers and unfortunately your order was damaged. We're receiving new stock tomorrow and will contact you with a new delivery date. I'm hoping to confirm a new date next week.

We're very sorry about the inconvenience caused, and would like to assure you that you'll receive your order as soon as possible. If you'd prefer to cancel your order, you can do so online. Do not hesitate to contact me if you have any questions.

Best wishes,

Janice Wright

What is Janice informing Yasmin about?

She is informing her that her order is delayed.

① What happened to the delivery van?

_____

② When is the company receiving new stock?

_____

③ What is Janice hoping to do next week?

_____

④ How can Yasmin cancel her order?

_____

⑤ Who should Yasmin contact if she has questions?

_____

Aa 11.4 MATCH THE DEFINITIONS TO THE CORRECT VERBS

to make a promise → to assure

① to delay doing something

② to favor one thing above another

③ to get or find something

④ to say something will definitely happen

⑤ to tell someone something

⑥ to call or email someone

⑦ to ask for something

to prefer

to confirm

to assure

to contact

to request

to hesitate

to inform

to obtain

11.5 KEY LANGUAGE CONTINUOUS TENSES FOR POLITENESS

In correspondence with clients, English often uses continuous tenses to make requests more polite or promises less specific.

PRESENT CONTINUOUS

We are hoping to deliver your order next Monday.

[We intend to deliver your order next Monday.]

PAST CONTINUOUS

The past continuous is only used for politeness here.

I was wondering if we could meet at your office.

[Let's meet at your office.]

FUTURE CONTINUOUS

Use "will," "be," and the verb with "-ing" to form the future continuous.

Will you be attending the launch of our soft drink range?

[We hope you will go to the launch.]

Aa 11.6 REWRITE THE HIGHLIGHTED PHRASES, CORRECTING THE ERRORS

To: Tyson Bailey

Subject: Poster campaign update

Dear Tyson Bailey,

Thanks for your email of December 12th regarding your poster campaign. I aiming to have a final meeting with the designers tomorrow morning, and I is hoping to send you more designs tomorrow afternoon.

We are currently wait for feedback from our focus group, but we expecting to hear from them soon. I was wonder if we could meet at your office to discuss their findings. I ensure you that we doing will be all we can to ensure that the campaign is completed on time. In the meantime, if you have any questions, please do not hesitate contacting me.

Yours,

Darius Gad

I am aiming to have _____

1 _____

2 _____

3 _____

4 _____

5 _____

6 _____

7 _____

11.7 REWRITE THE SENTENCES, CORRECTING THE ERRORS

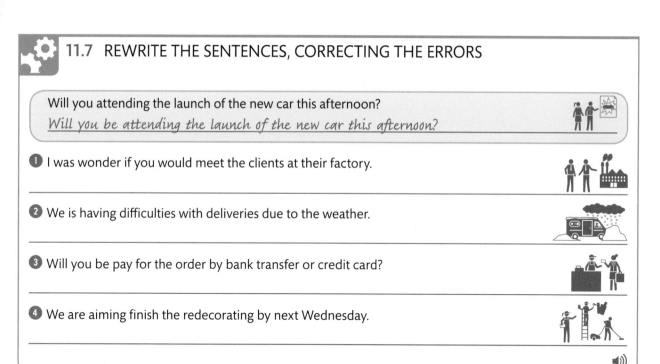

Will you attending the launch of the new car this afternoon?
Will you be attending the launch of the new car this afternoon?

1 I was wonder if you would meet the clients at their factory.

2 We is having difficulties with deliveries due to the weather.

3 Will you be pay for the order by bank transfer or credit card?

4 We are aiming finish the redecorating by next Wednesday.

11.8 REWRITE THE SENTENCES, PUTTING THE WORDS IN THE CORRECT ORDER

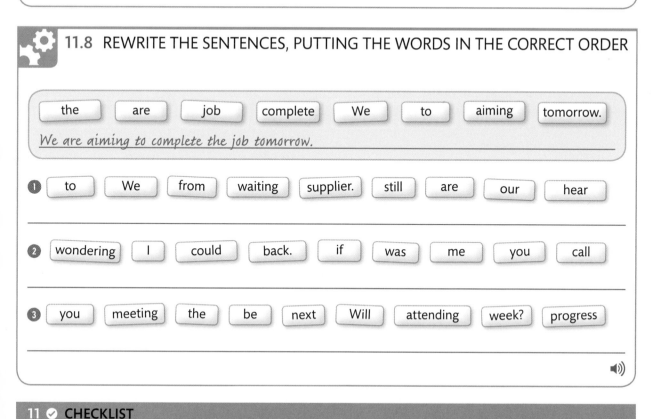

| the | are | job | complete | We | to | aiming | tomorrow. |

We are aiming to complete the job tomorrow.

1 | to | We | from | waiting | supplier. | still | are | our | hear |

2 | wondering | I | could | back. | if | was | me | you | call |

3 | you | meeting | the | be | next | Will | attending | week? | progress |

11 ✓ CHECKLIST

⚙ Continuous tenses ☐   **Aa** Arrangements and schedules ☐   👥 Keeping clients informed ☐

47

12 Informal communication

Phrasal verbs have two or more parts. They are often used in informal spoken and written English, in things such as messages and requests to co-workers.

⚙️ **New language** Phrasal verbs
Aa Vocabulary Arrangements and plans
🧩 **New skill** Keeping co-workers informed

12.1 KEY LANGUAGE PHRASAL VERBS

Phrasal verbs consist of a verb followed by at least one particle. Most particles in phrasal verbs are prepositions, and the particle often changes the meaning of the verb.

Verb   Particle

The paper in the copier has run out.

The particle often changes the meaning of the verb.

12.2 FURTHER EXAMPLES PHRASAL VERBS

 Could you look into fixing the coffee machine, please?

Welcome back! When would you like to catch up?

 Can you deal with the overseas orders?

I'm afraid I have to hang up now.

12.3 CROSS OUT THE INCORRECT WORDS IN EACH SENTENCE

When should we catch up / ~~off~~ / ~~out~~?

1. I'll look out / up / into the problem now.

2. The printer has run in / out / on of ink.

3. I need to catch / deal / look up with you.

4. Sorry, I have to hang in / up / into now.

5. Could you deal up / out / with this order?

6. I'll see / look / watch into Mr. Li's query.

7. My client just hung / run / ran up on me!

48

Nicky leaves a telephone message for her co-worker, Oscar.

Ⓐ I've got lots to do, so I have to hang up now. ☐

Ⓑ When one printer runs out of ink, all the others stop working, too. ☐

Ⓒ It would be nice to meet up sometime soon. ☐

Ⓓ I just wanted to catch up with you about your problem with the printers. ☑ 1

Ⓔ I looked into it a bit deeper and discovered the problem. ☐

Ⓕ It's quite easy to deal with. ☐

Aa 12.5 READ THE EMAIL AND MATCH THE PHRASAL VERBS TO THEIR DEFINITIONS

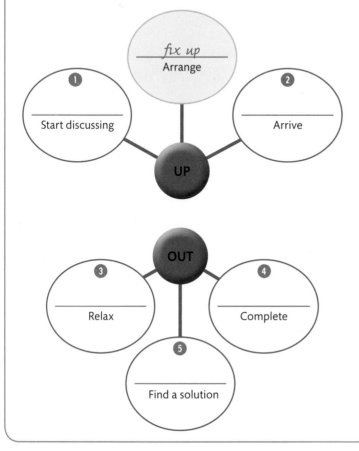

fix up
Arrange

① _____ Start discussing

② _____ Arrive

UP

OUT

③ _____ Relax

④ _____ Complete

⑤ _____ Find a solution

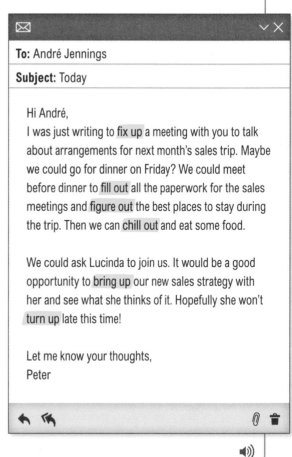

To: André Jennings

Subject: Today

Hi André,
I was just writing to fix up a meeting with you to talk about arrangements for next month's sales trip. Maybe we could go for dinner on Friday? We could meet before dinner to fill out all the paperwork for the sales meetings and figure out the best places to stay during the trip. Then we can chill out and eat some food.

We could ask Lucinda to join us. It would be a good opportunity to bring up our new sales strategy with her and see what she thinks of it. Hopefully she won't turn up late this time!

Let me know your thoughts,
Peter

12.6 KEY LANGUAGE SEPARABLE PHRASAL VERBS

With some phrasal verbs, the object of the sentence can go before or after the particle. The meaning is the same.

The object can go after the particle.

Please could you fill out this form?

Please could you fill this form out?

The object can come between the verb and the particle.

12.7 FURTHER EXAMPLES SEPARABLE PHRASAL VERBS

We have to back up our files every night.
We have to back our files up every night.

Sue's sick today. Let's call off the meeting.
Sue's sick today. Let's call the meeting off.

They're giving out samples of their products.
They're giving samples of their products out.

Please pass on the message to Jess.
Please pass the message on to Jess.

12.8 REWRITE THE SENTENCES BY CHANGING THE POSITION OF THE PARTICLE

Can we call off today's meeting?
Can we call today's meeting off?

❶ James, can you pass the message on to Zane?

_____

❷ Welcome to Jo's. Please fill out the visitor's form.

_____

❸ Can you stand at the exit and hand out the leaflets?

_____

❹ Put on a helmet before entering the site.

_____

❺ Before I update the software, back up your files.

_____

12.9 SAY THE SENTENCES OUT LOUD, FILLING IN THE GAPS USING THE WORDS IN THE PANEL

Every hour I ___back___ my new files ___up___ on my computer.

3 Howard, we should really _____ a meeting _____ for this week.

1 Could you please _____ the message _____ to Gary?

4 After a busy day in the office, I usually _____ _____ at home.

2 I have an important meeting, so I _____ a suit _____ this morning.

put	chill	~~back~~	on	out
pass	fix	up	on	~~up~~

🔊

12 ✓ CHECKLIST

⚙ Phrasal verbs ☐   **Aa** Arrangements and plans ☐   🧩 Keeping co-workers informed ☐

♻ REVIEW THE ENGLISH YOU HAVE LEARNED IN UNITS 7-12

NEW LANGUAGE	SAMPLE SENTENCE	☑	UNIT
PAST PERFECT AND PAST SIMPLE	**Sales of our products** had fallen, **so we** hired **a new marketing team.**	☐	7.1
PROJECT REPORTS	The following report presents **the results of a client satisfaction survey.**	☐	7.6
TELEPHONE APOLOGIES	I'm very sorry **about the delay.** Let's see what we can do.	☐	8.1
PRESENT PERFECT CONTINUOUS	**Our delivery company** has been experiencing **difficulties recently.**	☐	8.5
EMAILS TO CO-WORKERS	Please see **the timetable for next week's training course** attached.	☐	10.1
CONTINUOUS TENSES	We are hoping **to give you a full update.** I was wondering **if we could meet next week.**	☐	11.1, 11.5
PHRASAL VERBS	**The paper in the copier has** run out. **Could you please** fill **this form** out?	☐	12.1, 12.6

13.1 PRODUCTION

Everyone on the production line starts and finishes work at the same time.

a production line
[a line of people or machinery in a factory, each making a specific part of a product]

That car was unique. It was a one-off production for a private customer.

a one-off production
[something that is made or produced only once]

The price goes up as the cost of raw materials increases.

raw materials
[the basic substances that are used to make a product]

We can make changes. This is just a prototype.

a prototype
[the first form of a design that can be changed, copied, or developed]

These cars have become much cheaper with mass production.

mass production
[the process of making large numbers of goods, usually in a factory]

These fabrics are much cheaper to manufacture abroad.

to manufacture
[to make a large number of goods, usually in a factory and using machinery]

The bags are expensive because they are all handmade.

handmade
[made by a person without the use of a machine]

The overproduction of these shirts has meant we need to lower the price.

overproduction
[manufacturing too much of something in relation to demand]

All our toys go through a process of product testing.

product testing
[a process to check that goods meet certain standards]

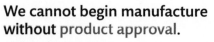

We cannot begin manufacture without product approval.

product approval
[a declaration that a product meets certain standards and is suitable for sale]

The packaging of certain goods is vital for sales.

packaging
[the external wrapping of goods before they are sold]

We arrange shipping all over the world for our clients.

shipping
[moving goods from one place to another]

The painting process starts in this room and takes two days.

a process
[a series of actions or steps that are done in a particular order]

These watches are beautiful, but their production is very labor intensive.

labor intensive
[requiring a lot of human effort to make something]

All the ingredients for this product are ethically sourced.

ethically sourced
[found or bought in a morally acceptable way]

Can you ask the warehouse how many we have available to ship today?

a warehouse
[a place where goods are stored before being shipped to customers or sellers]

We have a lot of stock. We need to sell it before we produce any more.

stock
[goods that a company has made but not yet sold]

With food products, quality control is vital.

quality control
[systems that ensure that products are of a high standard]

The factory makes 200,000 bars of chocolate a day.

a factory
[a building or group of buildings where goods are made]

They have been our main supplier of light bulbs for 20 years.

a supplier
[a company that provides or supplies another company with goods and services]

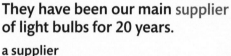

14 Describing a process

The passive voice can be useful when you need to describe how a process works. It emphasizes the action rather than the person or thing doing it.

⚙ **New language** The passive voice
Aa Vocabulary Processes and manufacturing
🧩 **New skill** Discussing how things are done

14.1 KEY LANGUAGE TALKING ABOUT PROCESSES WITH THE PASSIVE VOICE

The present simple passive is formed using "am / is / are" and the past participle.

Our products are designed in London.

The present simple passive describes current or routine events.

The present continuous passive is formed using "am / is / are" plus "being" and the past participle.

The new models are being released before Christmas.

The present continuous passive describes ongoing actions.

The present perfect passive is formed using "have / has" plus "been" and the past participle.

All the latest technologies have been used.

The present perfect passive describes past events that still have an effect on the present.

The past simple passive is formed using "was / were" and the past participle.

Our original model was sold worldwide.

The past simple passive describes a single completed action in the past.

The past continuous passive is formed using "was / were" plus "being" and the past participle.

We tested extensively while it was being redesigned.

The past continuous passive describes ongoing actions in the past.

The past perfect passive is formed using "had been" and the past participle.

The past perfect passive describes events that took place before another past event.

The media had been notified before we announce the launch.

🔊

14.2 READ THE ARTICLE AND ANSWER THE QUESTIONS

> Potato chips were invented over 100 years ago.
> **True** ✓ **False** ☐ **Not given** ☐

1 Chosen potatoes are kept at a steady temperature.
True ☐ **False** ☐ **Not given** ☐

2 The biggest potatoes make the best potato chips.
True ☐ **False** ☐ **Not given** ☐

3 Potato chips have never come in plastic packaging.
True ☐ **False** ☐ **Not given** ☐

4 Chip companies make more money now than ever.
True ☐ **False** ☐ **Not given** ☐

5 Chip companies do not monitor packaging styles.
True ☐ **False** ☐ **Not given** ☐

BUSINESS TODAY

A slice of history

**The essential potato chip:
How did we get here?**

It is believed that the first potato chips were created at the end of the 19th century. But how are they made? First, golf-ball-sized potatoes are chosen and stored at a constant temperature. The potatoes are then sliced and fried, and additives are used to keep the chips fresh. Potato-chip packaging has been constantly changing. Packets have been made from paper, foil, plastic, and newer, composite materials. The quality of modern packaging is our main focus and is constantly being monitored.

 14.3 CROSS OUT THE INCORRECT WORDS IN EACH SENTENCE

> We make everything on site at the Imagicorp plant. All of our products are built / ~~build~~ in Europe.

1 Over the last year, an exciting new line has been developed / develop.

2 This design has been / was patented in 1938. Nobody has ever managed to make a better product!

3 Their new line is being / have been launched next Saturday. Everyone is talking about it.

4 Our factory floor was / is being cleaned before the CEO visited. He was happy things looked good!

5 You don't need to worry about dinner. The food is / had been cooked to order so that it is fresh.

6 The first cars made in this factory were / was sold in the UK in 1972, and worldwide the next year.

7 Our original designers has been / were influenced by Japanese artists.

8 To prepare for the launch, advertising posters are / are being put up around town as we speak.

14.4 KEY LANGUAGE AGENTS IN THE PASSIVE VOICE

"By" can be used to show the person
or thing doing the action.

Our CEO will announce the launch soon.

This active sentence emphasizes the
person doing the action ("our CEO").

The launch will be announced soon.

In the passive sentence, the action is
emphasized and "the launch" is the subject.

The launch will be announced soon by our CEO.

"By" is added to show the person doing the action,
while still emphasizing the action itself.

14.5 HOW TO FORM AGENTS IN THE PASSIVE VOICE

SUBJECT	FORM OF "BE"	PAST PARTICIPLE	REST OF SENTENCE	"BY"
The launch	will be	announced	soon	by our CEO.

14.6 FILL IN THE GAPS USING THE PASSIVE PHRASES IN THE PANEL

How many new models ____*are being produced*____ ?

1 Their new products _____ on TV now.

2 80,000 packets _____ in the factory each week.

3 A thousand new cars _____ next week.

4 Our latest gadget _____ by Ronnie Angel.

5 The production line _____ during the summer.

6 Great advances in design _____ recently.

are being promoted

~~are being produced~~

are produced

is stopped

will be sold

have been made

was invented

14.7 REWRITE THE SENTENCES USING THE PASSIVE VOICE, USING "BY" TO SHOW THE AGENT

> Our promotions team markets the product worldwide.
> *The product is marketed worldwide by our promotions team.*

1 Someone checks all the cars before they leave the factory.

_____

2 Maxine invented the new photo app for professional artists.

_____

3 Customers bought all Carl Osric's books on the publication date.

_____

4 Ron buys all our vegetarian ingredients from the market.

_____

5 Samantha checks all of the invoices before they are sent out.

_____

14.8 LISTEN TO THE AUDIO, THEN NUMBER THE PICTURES IN THE ORDER THEY ARE DESCRIBED

A ☐

B 1

C ☐

D ☐
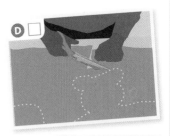

E ☐

F ☐

G ☐

H ☐

14.9 KEY LANGUAGE MODALS IN THE PASSIVE VOICE

Certain modals can be used as set phrases in the passive voice to express ideas such as possibility, ability, likelihood, and obligation.

The importance of product testing can't be overestimated.

[Product testing is very important.]

All products must be approved before leaving the factory.

[Products have to meet certain standards before they leave the factory.]

The product must have been damaged before it was shipped.

[It seems very likely that the product was broken before it was shipped.]

The shipment could have been packaged more carefully.

[The shipment was not packed as carefully as it should have been.]

This device couldn't have been tested before it went on sale.

[It seems impossible that the device was tested before it was sold.]

 ## 14.10 MATCH THE ACTIVE SENTENCES TO THE PASSIVE SENTENCES WITH THE SAME MEANING

We must not ignore the costs.	This picture couldn't have been drawn by Sanjit.
❶ Tim must have bought these flowers today.	The price shouldn't have been accepted.
❷ You can't mark these down yet. They're new.	The costs can't be ignored.
❸ Sanjit could not have drawn this picture.	These glasses must be packaged carefully.
❹ Niamh shouldn't have accepted the price.	They can't be marked down yet! They're new.
❺ You should package these glasses carefully.	The oven has been turned up.
❻ Nobody should ignore faults in the products.	These flowers must have been bought today.
❼ Someone has turned the oven up.	Faults in the product shouldn't be ignored.

14.11 SAY THE SENTENCES OUT LOUD, FILLING IN THE GAPS USING THE WORDS IN THE PANEL

How It's Made

A look at an electric car assembly line.

First, the component parts ___*are delivered*___ to separate parts of the factory.

❶ The chassis parts are placed on the _____ .

❷ The engine and radiator _____ by a robot as they are very heavy.

❸ The engine and radiator _____ to the chassis by an assembly worker.

❹ The bodywork is fully _____ on a separate line.

❺ The assembled bodywork is inspected before _____ by a robot.

❻ The chassis and bodywork are joined together before the vehicle _____ .

being painted	is checked	~~are delivered~~	assembly line
assembled and welded		are secured	are lifted

14 ✓ CHECKLIST

⚙ The passive voice ☐   **Aa** Processes and manufacturing ☐   🧩 Discussing how things are done ☐

15 Describing a product

When describing a product, you will usually use adjectives. You can use more that one adjective, but they must be in a particular order.

🔧 **New language** Adjective order
Aa Vocabulary Opinion and fact adjectives
🧩 **New skill** Describing a product

15.1 KEY LANGUAGE ADJECTIVE ORDER

The meaning of an adjective decides its order in a sentence. Opinions come first, followed by different types of facts.

Fact adjectives also have their own order, depending on their meaning.

OPINION ADJECTIVE   FACT ADJECTIVES   NOUN

Look at this fantastic huge plastic model!

SIZE   MATERIAL

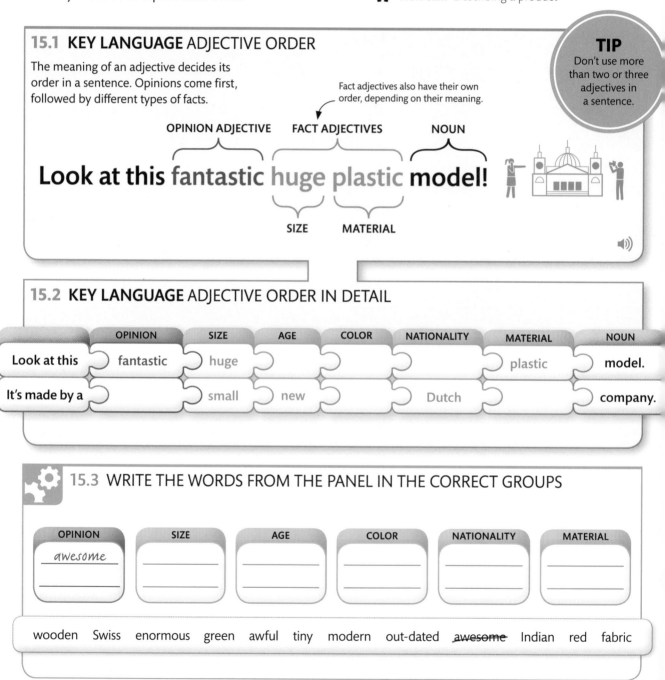

TIP
Don't use more than two or three adjectives in a sentence.

15.2 KEY LANGUAGE ADJECTIVE ORDER IN DETAIL

	OPINION	SIZE	AGE	COLOR	NATIONALITY	MATERIAL	NOUN
Look at this	fantastic	huge				plastic	**model.**
It's made by a		small	new		Dutch		**company.**

15.3 WRITE THE WORDS FROM THE PANEL IN THE CORRECT GROUPS

OPINION	SIZE	AGE	COLOR	NATIONALITY	MATERIAL
awesome					

wooden   Swiss   enormous   green   awful   tiny   modern   out-dated   ~~awesome~~   Indian   red   fabric

15.4 REWRITE THE SENTENCES, PUTTING THE WORDS IN THE CORRECT ORDER

| I | this | blue | version! | new, | love |

I love this new, blue version!

① | the | you | plastic | seen | Have | desks? | ugly, |

_____

② | metallic | We're | range | new, | launching | the | tomorrow. |

_____

③ | you | Would | diamond | prefer | ones? | these | tiny, |

_____

15.5 LISTEN TO THE AUDIO AND MARK WHICH THINGS ARE DESCRIBED

61

15.6 KEY LANGUAGE SPECIFIC AND GENERAL OPINIONS

General opinion adjectives always come before specific ones. General opinion adjectives can describe lots of different things. Specific opinion adjectives can only usually describe a certain type of thing.

OPINION ADJECTIVES   FACT ADJECTIVE

What a nice, friendly new team!

"Nice" is a general opinion adjective. It can describe lots of different things.

"Friendly" is a specific opinion adjective. It usually only describes people or animals.

15.7 CROSS OUT THE INCORRECT WORD IN EACH SENTENCE

Our catering team is developing a fantastic, ~~friendly~~ / delicious menu for the conference.

1 I'm interested in that incredible / French modern device we saw at the sales fair.

2 Our competitors are still selling those really blue / ugly, large cotton shirts.

3 The office has a profitable / friendly, old black cat that visits regularly.

4 Frances, have you seen these Peruvian silver / small earrings that I brought back?

5 Did you get one of those new plastic / fantastic business cards?

6 A lot of customers have been asking for the new / German red version.

7 My boss has asked me to design a small, paper / fantastic package for the product.

8 I have bought some new leather / large chairs for the boardroom.

15.8 READ THE ARTICLE AND ANSWER THE QUESTIONS

White guest towels are cheaper this year.
True ☐ **False** ☐ **Not given** ✓

① The Festival towel range is colorful.
True ☐ **False** ☐ **Not given** ☐

② There is a discount on Festival towels.
True ☐ **False** ☐ **Not given** ☐

③ Black tablecloths are a new product.
True ☐ **False** ☐ **Not given** ☐

④ The kitchen towels are made of paper.
True ☐ **False** ☐ **Not given** ☐

⑤ The kitchen towels are made in Egypt.
True ☐ **False** ☐ **Not given** ☐

LARA'S LINEN

We have everything your hotel or restaurant needs, from guest towels through to tablecloths. We are keeping our wonderful, best-selling white guest towels at the same fantastic price as last year. But this year we are also adding a range of stunning, multicolored "Festival" towels to our Hotel range. We are also adding to our wonderful Egyptian cotton tableware range. As well as the usual black and white ranges, we now offer burgundy, brown, and olive-colored tablecloths and napkins. Don't forget to check out our hard-wearing, Turkish, cotton kitchen towels and aprons in the Kitchen section of the brochure.

15.9 SAY THE SENTENCES OUT LOUD, FILLING IN THE GAPS USING THE WORDS IN THE PANEL

His marketing strategy is a
fantastic , intelligent idea.

① We offer great, _____
food that people can afford.

② Look at that _____ new
billboard across the street.

③ I love buying _____ wooden
furniture for the office.

④ My boss drives a tiny _____ car
to work. It's definitely easy to spot!

⑤ We aim to offer awesome, _____
customer service at all times.

| delicious | enormous | ~~fantastic~~ |
| friendly | green | antique |

15 ✓ CHECKLIST

⚙ Adjective order ☐   **Aa** Fact and opinion adjectives ☐   🧩 Describing a product ☐

16.1 MARKETING AND ADVERTISING

advertising agency

advertisement / ad

copywriter

write copy

brand

logo

slogan / tagline

unique selling point / USP

promote

publicity

press release

door-to-door sales

poster

billboard

sponsor

merchandise

consumer

market research

sales pitch

free sample

special offer

leaflet / flyer

direct mail

coupons

online marketing

online survey

social media

word of mouth

television advertising

radio advertising

telemarketing

small ads / personal ads

17 Marketing a product

You can use a variety of adjectives and adverbs to describe the key features when marketing a product or service. Not all adjectives can be modified in the same way.

🔧 **New language** Adjectives and adverbs
Aa Vocabulary Descriptive adjectives
🧩 **New skill** Modifying descriptions of products

17.1 KEY LANGUAGE NON-GRADABLE ADJECTIVES

Most adjectives are known as "gradable" adjectives. They can be modified with grading adverbs, such as "slightly," "very," and "extremely." Non-gradable adjectives cannot be modified in this way.

Our products are good.

Gradable adjectives like "good" can be modified with grading adverbs like "extremely" and "very."

Yes, they're extremely good.

Non-gradable adjectives like "fantastic" cannot be modified by grading adverbs.

I think they're fantastic!

17.2 FURTHER EXAMPLES NON-GRADABLE ADJECTIVES

Non-gradable adjectives fall into three categories: extreme, absolute, and classifying.

The demand is enormous.

Extreme adjectives are stronger versions of gradable adjectives. "Enormous" has the sense of "extremely big."

They have a unique design.

Absolute adjectives like "unique" describe fixed qualities or states.

Our customer base is American.

Classifying adjectives are used to say that something is of a specific class or type.

17.3 WRITE THE ADJECTIVES FROM THE PANEL IN THE CORRECT CATEGORIES

EXTREME	ABSOLUTE	CLASSIFYING
awful	_unique_	_organic_
_____ _____	_____ _____	_____ _____
_____ _____	_____ _____	_____ _____

fantastic	~~awful~~	impossible	tiny	right	digital	~~organic~~	disgusting
perfect	industrial	wrong	electronic	~~unique~~	enormous	chemical	

🔊

17.4 READ THE ARTICLE AND ANSWER THE QUESTIONS

The author owns his own marketing company.
True ☐ **False** ☐ **Not given** ☑

① Give readers a reason for buying your product.
True ☐ **False** ☐ **Not given** ☐

② Deals of the Day can encourage people to buy.
True ☐ **False** ☐ **Not given** ☐

③ Put key words in a different color text.
True ☐ **False** ☐ **Not given** ☐

④ The article only talks about newsletters.
True ☐ **False** ☐ **Not given** ☐

⑤ Readers do not trust the words "Free" and "New."
True ☐ **False** ☐ **Not given** ☐

⑥ The article recommends setting up a website.
True ☐ **False** ☐ **Not given** ☐

Writing for buyers

Rachid Barbery talks about writing effective marketing texts

LIMITED OFFER

DEAL OF THE DAY

Research has shown that there are certain techniques you can use to turn your readers into buyers. First, repeat the positive facts about the product to make them more believable. Make sure you explain why readers would benefit from buying your product compared to others. For example, say that your digital camera weighs 100g less than similar ones and has a unique rubber grip because it makes it easier to carry when traveling. Use the word "you" a lot to help make the connection between the reader and the product. It's also a good idea to promote limited time offers or limited editions as these create an extra reason to buy your product now. This could be a Deal of the Day or Special Edition Color. Using key words in your newsletters and the front pages of your websites or leaflets, such as "Free" and "New" always creates interest and a positive response in readers.

17.5 KEY LANGUAGE NON-GRADING ADVERBS

Some adverbs can be used to qualify non-gradable
adjectives. These are called "non-grading adverbs,"
and often mean "entirely" or "almost entirely."
They cannot usually be used with gradable adjectives.

The demand is
absolutely **enormous!**

They have a totally
new **design.**

Our customer base is
completely **American.**

17.6 FURTHER EXAMPLES NON-GRADING ADVERBS

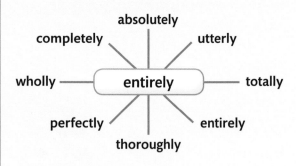

absolutely
completely — utterly
wholly — **entirely** — totally
perfectly — entirely
thoroughly

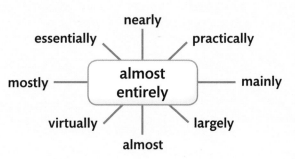

nearly
essentially — practically
mostly — **almost entirely** — mainly
virtually — largely
almost

17.7 MARK THE SENTENCES THAT ARE CORRECT

The product is utterly good. ☐
The product is utterly amazing. ☑

❶ The new gadget is completely digital. ☐
The new gadget is completely bad. ☐

❷ This draft design is practically perfect. ☐
This draft design is practically all right. ☐

❸ The client said it was totally fantastic. ☐
The client said it was totally nice. ☐

❹ His decision to invest was entirely right. ☐
His decision to invest was maybe right. ☐

❺ This area of town is largely industrial. ☐
This area of town is large industrial. ☐

17.8 KEY LANGUAGE "REALLY," "FAIRLY," AND "PRETTY"

A few adverbs can be used with both gradable and non-gradable
adjectives. They are "really" (meaning "very much"), and "pretty"
and "fairly" (both meaning "quite a lot, but not very").

TIP
Note that "fairly"
can have a negative
connotation and so is not
normally used to suggest
something is very good
or necessary.

Gradable

What you need is a really $\left\{ \begin{array}{c} \text{good} \\ \text{brilliant} \end{array} \right\}$ **idea.**

Non-gradable

You need to be fairly $\left\{ \begin{array}{c} \text{confident} \\ \text{certain} \end{array} \right\}$ **it works.**

Inventing a new product is pretty $\left\{ \begin{array}{c} \text{difficult} \\ \text{impossible} \end{array} \right\}$.

17.9 LISTEN TO THE AUDIO AND ANSWER THE QUESTIONS

Two marketing executives
are discussing products at
a trade fair.

Sales of Vietnamese instant meals are...
quite poor. ☐
fairly good. ☐
really good. ☑

❶ The target market for the instant
meal range is...
mainly European. ☐
entirely European. ☐
mostly Asian. ☐

❷ How does Marion feel about selling to the
European market?
Really confident ☐
Pretty confident ☐
Totally confident ☐

❸ What does Sean think about the
taste of the meals?
Fairly tasty ☐
Pretty tasty ☐
Absolutely delicious ☐

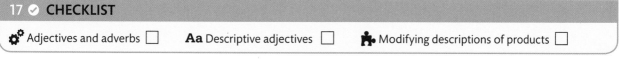

17 ✔ CHECKLIST

⚙ Adjectives and adverbs ☐   **Aa** Descriptive adjectives ☐   🧩 Modifying descriptions of products ☐

18 Advertising and branding

When you want to tell people about your company, product, or brand, intensifiers like "enough," "too," "so," and "such" can help communicate your point.

⚙ **New language** Intensifiers
Aa Vocabulary "Enough," "too," "so," and "such"
🧩 **New skill** Adding emphasis to descriptions

18.1 KEY LANGUAGE "ENOUGH" AND "TOO"

"Enough" can be used after an adjective or adverb to show that it's the right degree.

Our warehouse is big enough for your needs.

Adjective + "enough"

We always package items safely enough for delivery.

Adverb + "enough"

"Too" can be used before an adjective or adverb to show that it's more than enough.

"Too" + adjective

"Too" + adverb

Their product is too expensive. Nobody will buy it.

The motor runs too loudly. It's really unpleasant.

🔊

18.2 MARK THE SENTENCES THAT ARE CORRECT

The shipping cost is too high. ☑
The shipping cost is enough high. ☐

❶ Is the office big enough for us? ☐
Is the office enough big for us? ☐

❷ The delivery times are too slowly. ☐
The delivery times are too slow. ☐

❸ Are these shelves strong enough? ☐
Are these shelves too strong? ☐

🔊

18.3 LISTEN TO THE AUDIO AND MARK WHICH THINGS ARE DESCRIBED

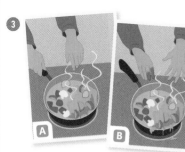

 18.4 READ THE ARTICLE AND ANSWER THE QUESTIONS

The ad suggests images are often too small.
True ☐ **False** ☐ **Not given** ☑

1 Over half of clients view websites on computers.
True ☐ **False** ☐ **Not given** ☐

2 A poor website could mean you lose customers.
True ☐ **False** ☐ **Not given** ☐

3 50% of consumers shop online.
True ☐ **False** ☐ **Not given** ☐

4 Mobiopt Web focuses on what the website looks like and how it works.
True ☐ **False** ☐ **Not given** ☐

5 You have to pay Mobiopt Web for a quote.
True ☐ **False** ☐ **Not given** ☐

Mobiopt Web

HOME | PORTFOLIO | ABOUT | CONTACT

What we do

Have you ever considered what your website looks like on a mobile device? Is the text big enough to read? Are the images too small to showcase your fantastic products? Research says that over 50 percent of your potential clients are likely to use mobile devices to view your site. You need it to look and work perfectly on these devices, otherwise your customer may soon become someone else's.

At Mobiopt Web, we work with you to ensure that not only does your website look great, but that it also does exactly what you and your clients want it to.

Contact us now for a free quotation on your new web design.

18.5 KEY LANGUAGE "SO" AND "SUCH"

"Such" can be added before a noun to add emphasis. It can also be added before an adjective and noun combination.

TIP
"Such" + "a / an" + noun is more common with extreme nouns such as "success" rather than neutral ones such as "event."

The new model was such a success.

"Such" + "a/an" + noun

It was such an important meeting.

"Such" + "a/an" + adjective + noun

"So" can be added before an adjective or an adverb to add emphasis.

Initial reviews are so important.

"So" + adjective

The product launch went so well!

"So" + adverb

18.6 REWRITE THE SENTENCES, PUTTING THE WORDS IN THE CORRECT ORDER

| price | The | high! | so | is |

The price is so high!

4 | My | so | is | ambitious. | boss |

_____

1 | such | It's | a | product. | great |

_____

5 | phones | so | cheap. | Their | are |

_____

2 | boring. | was | so | meeting | The |

_____

6 | so | Her | is | company | big! |

_____

3 | such | His | was | surprise. | news | a |

_____

7 | surprise! | was | such | Our | launch | a |

_____

18.7 CROSS OUT THE INCORRECT WORD IN EACH SENTENCE, THEN SAY THE SENTENCES OUT LOUD

There is such / ~~so~~ a big crowd at the trade fair this year!

❶ The slogan is far such / too complicated. We need to simplify it.

❷ They have created such / enough a brilliant poster campaign.

❸ We haven't done too / enough market research. We need to understand our consumers.

❹ Our supervisor is such / too a creative person. She designed our new logo.

❺ Marion is such / so persuasive when she delivers a sales pitch.

---

18 ✓ CHECKLIST

⚙ Intensifiers ☐   Aa "Enough," "too," "so," and "such" ☐   🧩 Adding emphasis to descriptions ☐

♻ REVIEW THE ENGLISH YOU HAVE LEARNED IN UNITS 13–18

NEW LANGUAGE	SAMPLE SENTENCE	☑	UNIT
DESCRIBING A PROCESS WITH THE PASSIVE VOICE	Our products are designed in London. Our original model was sold worldwide.	☐	14.1
DESCRIBING A PRODUCT WITH CORRECT ADJECTIVE ORDER	Look at this fantastic, huge plastic model!	☐	15.1, 15.2
SPECIFIC AND GENERAL OPINIONS	What a nice, friendly new team!	☐	15.6
NON-GRADABLE ADJECTIVES AND NON-GRADING ADVERBS	They have a new design. They have a totally new design.	☐	17.1 17.5
"ENOUGH" AND "TOO"	Our warehouse is big enough for your needs. Their product is too expensive.	☐	18.1
"SO" AND "SUCH" FOR EMPHASIS	The new model was such a success. Initial reviews are so important.	☐	18.5

19 Advice and suggestions

English uses modal verbs such as "could," "should," and "must" for advice or suggestions. They can be used to help co-workers in difficult or stressful situations.

⚙ **New language** Modal verbs for advice
Aa Vocabulary Workplace pressures
🧩 **New skill** Giving advice

19.1 KEY LANGUAGE GIVING ADVICE

English uses "could," "should," and "must" to vary the strength of advice given.

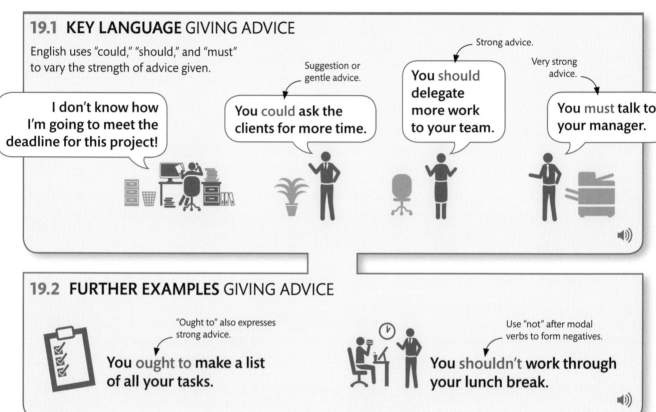

I don't know how I'm going to meet the deadline for this project!

Suggestion or gentle advice.
You could ask the clients for more time.

Strong advice.
You should delegate more work to your team.

Very strong advice.
You must talk to your manager.

19.2 FURTHER EXAMPLES GIVING ADVICE

"Ought to" also expresses strong advice.
You ought to make a list of all your tasks.

Use "not" after modal verbs to form negatives.
You shouldn't work through your lunch break.

19.3 MATCH THE SITUATIONS TO THE CORRECT ADVICE

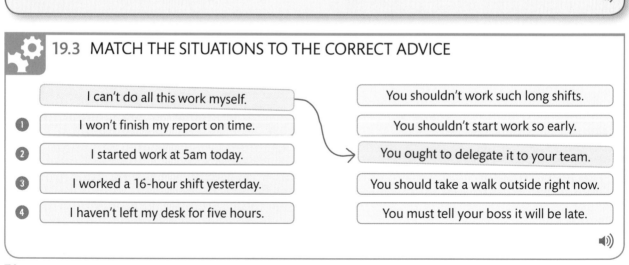

I can't do all this work myself.

1. I won't finish my report on time.
2. I started work at 5am today.
3. I worked a 16-hour shift yesterday.
4. I haven't left my desk for five hours.

You shouldn't work such long shifts.

You shouldn't start work so early.

You ought to delegate it to your team.

You should take a walk outside right now.

You must tell your boss it will be late.

19.4 FILL IN THE GAPS USING THE PHRASES IN THE PANEL

You really need a break. You _____*shouldn't take*_____ work home.

shouldn't take

ought to take

could try

shouldn't feel

must delegate

should stop

1 My wife said I _____ yoga and relaxation techniques.

2 You _____ working right away if you feel sick.

3 You _____ a break if you're really tired.

4 You _____ exhausted at the beginning of the week.

5 You _____ some of your work to your assistant.

19.5 REWRITE THE SENTENCES, CORRECTING THE ERRORS

You **ought** talk to your manager.
You ought to talk to your manager.

1 You **are ought** to relax more.

_____

2 You **must to stop** taking work home every day.

_____

3 He **could trying** to delegate more tasks.

_____

4 You **shouldn't to worry** so much about work.

_____

5 She **shoulds talk** to her colleagues.

_____

6 He **ought to quits** his job if he hates it.

_____

19.6 LISTEN TO THE AUDIO AND MARK WHETHER KATE ADVISES GIORGOS TO DO THE ACTIVITY IN EACH PICTURE

Yes ✓ No ☐

1 Yes ☐ No ☐

2 Yes ☐ No ☐

3 Yes ☐ No ☐

4 Yes ☐ No ☐

19.7 KEY LANGUAGE MAKING SUGGESTIONS

Use "What about...?" with a gerund or "Why don't we...?" with a base verb to make suggestions.

What about hiring
Why don't we hire } more staff?

19.8 HOW TO FORM SUGGESTIONS

"WHAT ABOUT"	GERUND	REST OF SENTENCE
What about	hiring	
"WHY DON'T WE"	BASE VERB	more staff?
Why don't we	hire	

19.9 FURTHER EXAMPLES MAKING SUGGESTIONS

 What about working **from home on Fridays?**

 Why don't we organize **a team lunch?**

 What about opening **a new store?**

 Why don't we file **these documents?**

19.10 USE THE CHART TO CREATE SIX CORRECT SENTENCES AND SAY THEM OUT LOUD

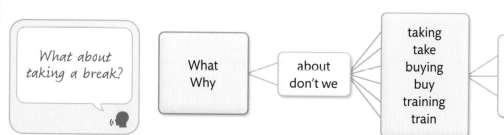

What about taking a break?

What	about	taking	a break?
Why	don't we	take	better equipment?
		buying	new employees?
		buy	
		training	
		train	

19.11 CROSS OUT THE INCORRECT WORD IN EACH SENTENCE

What about ~~train~~ / training our staff better?

1 Why don't we buy / buying new chairs?

2 Why don't we go / going for a walk outside?

3 What about drink / drinking less coffee?

4 Why don't we provide / providing free fruit?

5 What about make / making a list of your tasks?

6 What about delegate / delegating this to Jo?

7 Why don't we ask / asking Paul to help us?

19.12 READ THE ARTICLE AND ANSWER THE QUESTIONS

A heavy workload can affect your health.
True ☑ False ☐

1 You must find out what makes you stressed.
True ☐ False ☐

2 When you are stressed, you can concentrate.
True ☐ False ☐

3 Exercise can help you deal with stress.
True ☐ False ☐

4 You should work through your lunch break.
True ☐ False ☐

5 It's important to get a good night's sleep.
True ☐ False ☐

6 You shouldn't tell people how you feel.
True ☐ False ☐

YOUR HEALTH

Stressed out at work?

Our experts give advice about coping with a busy workload

To protect your health from the effects of a heavy workload, you must discover why you feel stressed at work. Then you should learn to recognize signs of excessive stress, such as:
• feeling depressed
• problems sleeping
• difficulty concentrating
• headaches.

Next, you ought to develop positive coping strategies such as exercising and eating well. Have a real break at lunchtime. This in turn will help you sleep better and longer. What about making your night-time routine and your bedroom more relaxing? Sleep is very important, so you shouldn't miss out on it. Finally, you should talk to others about your feelings.

---

19 ✔ CHECKLIST
⚙ Modal verbs for advice ☐   **Aa** Workplace pressures ☐   👥 Giving advice ☐

20 Vocabulary

20.1 MANAGEMENT AND LEADERSHIP

Every year I have an appraisal with my manager.

an appraisal / a performance review
[an interview to discuss an employee's performance]

We get a $500 sales bonus if we meet our targets.

a bonus
[money added to a person's wages as a reward for good performance]

I was promoted this year, so I have my own office.

to be promoted
[to be given a more senior position within a company]

My boss is really pleased with my performance this year.

performance
[how well a person carries out tasks]

20.2 SKILLS AND ABILITIES

organization

IT / computing

administration

problem-solving

numeracy

customer service

interpersonal skills

leadership

public speaking

written communication

initiative

telephone manner

Our manager has to approve this before it goes to the client.

to approve
[to officially confirm something meets the required standards]

I like to delegate tasks to give my co-workers a variety of work.

to delegate
[to give work or tasks to a person in a position junior to you]

My team leader allocates tasks at the beginning of each week.

to allocate a task
[to give a task to somebody]

I have to designate a colleague as the main first aider in the office.

to designate
[to choose somebody to take on a particular role]

data analysis

decision-making

teamwork

fast learner

research

fluent in languages

attention to detail

negotiating

work well under pressure

able to drive

project management

time management

21 Talking about abilities

To talk about people's skills, for example in a performance review, you can use various modal verbs to express present, past, and future ability.

⚙ **New language** Modal verbs for abilities
Aa Vocabulary Workplace skills
🧩 **New skill** Describing abilities

21.1 KEY LANGUAGE TALKING ABOUT PRESENT ABILITY

Use "can," "can't," and "cannot" to talk about people's skills and abilities in the present.

Jasmine's team **can finish** the job really quickly.

🔊

21.2 FURTHER EXAMPLES TALKING ABOUT PRESENT ABILITY

Umar **can create beautiful flower arrangements.**

I **can fix your car by the end of the day.**

Negative form of "can." English also uses "cannot."

Stuart **can't cook in a professional kitchen.**

They **can't work together without arguing.**

🔊

⚙ 21.3 FILL IN THE GAPS USING "CAN" OR "CAN'T"

Alastair has excellent IT skills. He _____*can*_____ create computer programs and apps.

1 She doesn't like meeting new people. She _____ work in the HR department.

2 Shaun _____ work really well with new employees, so he should help run our training course.

3 Have you seen her brilliant photographs? She _____ create our posters and flyers.

4 Lydia failed her driving test, so, unfortunately, she _____ drive the delivery van.

🔊

21.4 KEY LANGUAGE TALKING ABOUT PAST ABILITY

Use "could" to talk about abilities in the past.
The negative form is "couldn't" or "could not."

My old team could work really well, but my new team can't concentrate.

PAST

NOW

I used to be so nervous that I couldn't speak in public, but now I can give presentations.

PAST

NOW

21.5 REWRITE THE SENTENCES, CORRECTING THE ERRORS

For years she can't drive but now she has passed her test.

For years she couldn't drive but now she has passed her test.

① Peter can't use the new coffee machine. He didn't know how it worked.

② Varinder could write reports very well at first, but she can now that she's had more practice.

③ No one in the office can read his handwriting. It was awful.

④ Bill was the only person who can't figure out how to use the photocopier.

21.6 KEY LANGUAGE TALKING ABOUT FUTURE POTENTIAL

English uses "could" to talk about people's future abilities and potential. In this context, "could" can be followed by most English verbs.

Use "could" before most verbs to talk about possible future situations.

If Felipe keeps on working hard, he could become head chef.

Jenny could reach the top of our company's sales rankings.

You can also use "would" followed by "do," "make," or "be" to talk about future potential. "Would" is stronger than "could," and suggests that something is more likely to happen.

Use "do" or "make" after "would" to talk about future potential.

Kim is good at training people. She would make an excellent team leader.

Liz is really polite. She would do well in the customer services department.

21.7 MARK WHETHER THE STATEMENTS REFER TO PAST OR FUTURE ABILITY

> You could be head of your department.
> **Past** ☐ **Future** ☑

❶ She would make a great team leader.
  Past ☐ **Future** ☐

❷ He couldn't cook before his training.
  Past ☐ **Future** ☐

❸ He would do well in a smaller team.
  Past ☐ **Future** ☐

❹ Ray could get along with the old CEO.
  Past ☐ **Future** ☐

❺ Fiona could do better if she tried.
  Past ☐ **Future** ☐

Shona is having her annual performance review with her manager.

1 Nick is pleased with Shona's work.
True ☐ False ☐ Not given ☐

2 Shona has worked there for five years.
True ☐ False ☐ Not given ☐

3 Shona will get a $500 bonus.
True ☐ False ☐ Not given ☐

4 Shona can't work well with new staff.
True ☐ False ☐ Not given ☐

5 Shona wouldn't be a good team leader.
True ☐ False ☐ Not given ☐

Shona's manager wants to talk about her past.
True ☐ False ☐ Not given ☑

21.9 CROSS OUT THE INCORRECT WORD IN EACH SENTENCE, THEN SAY THE SENTENCES OUT LOUD

You're an excellent sales assistant, and you ~~can't~~ / would do well in the marketing team.

1 James's team was weak, but he's trained them well and now they can / can't do anything.

2 We think that you are really creative and couldn't / would make a great addition to the PR team.

3 I don't know what is wrong with me today. I can / can't get anything finished.

4 My confidence is much better now. Before, I would / couldn't talk in public.

---

21 ✓ CHECKLIST

⚙ Modal verbs for abilities ☐   **Aa** Workplace skills ☐   🧩 Describing abilities ☐

22 Comparing and contrasting

In team discussions, discourse markers can ease the flow of conversation. They can help link similar or contrasting ideas, or connect an action to a result.

⚙ **New language** Discourse markers
Aa Vocabulary Teamwork and team building
🧩 **New skill** Expressing your ideas

22.1 KEY LANGUAGE EXPRESSING SIMILAR IDEAS

Some discourse markers link ideas that are similar to each other.

This training is useful for your day-to-day work. It is **also** fun.

Team A completed the task very quickly. Team B were **equally** successful.

Laziness is a terrible trait for a team member. Dishonesty is very bad, **too**.

It is important to say what we all think. We should listen to each other **as well**.

22.2 KEY LANGUAGE EXPRESSING CONTRASTING IDEAS

Some discourse markers link contrasting ideas.

The training today was useful. **However,** yesterday's task was pointless.

Although Team A completed the task quickly, Team B didn't finish it.

Some people want to run a team, **while** others want to be team members.

Laziness is a terrible trait in a team, **whereas** hard work is excellent.

All staff should follow the dress code for the training. Please be on time, ~~while~~ / too.

 1 Although / **Equally** I attended the training session, I'm not sure I learned very much.

 2 You got a high score for the IT test, and you've done **equally** / while well on the team-building course.

 3 Team A built a small boat out of plastic bottles, **as well** / whereas Team B used wood to make theirs.

 4 The training day is a great way to learn new skills. It's **also** / however a good way to get to know people.

🔊

22.4 LISTEN TO THE AUDIO AND ANSWER THE QUESTIONS

  A team-building coach is giving feedback on two teams' performances.

The coach says the team-building days are...
challenging and tiring. ☐
challenging but rewarding. ☐
challenging and fun. ☑

1 At the beginning of the team-building day, the participants...
walked across bridges over a river. ☐
walked across bridges high in the air. ☐
made ladders to climb up trees. ☐

2 This task challenged the participants to...
overcome fear and help each other. ☐
deal with a fear of heights. ☐
learn how to build rope bridges. ☐

3 Members of Team Bear were...
the tallest and the quickest. ☐
the tallest and the most scared. ☐
the tallest, whereas Team Lion were slowest. ☐

4 Members of Team Bear helped each other while members of Team Lion...
disagreed with each other. ☐
worked too slowly. ☐
raced each other to the finish. ☐

5 In the future, Team Lion should...
help Team Bear to be less afraid. ☐
argue less and work faster. ☐
work more slowly and listen to their teammates. ☐

22.5 KEY LANGUAGE TALKING ABOUT RESULTS

Some discourse markers link an action or situation with its result.

Less formal discourse markers.

The training days are useful. { As a result, For this reason, Consequently, As a consequence, } **everyone attends them.**

More formal discourse markers.

22.6 MARK THE SENTENCES THAT ARE CORRECT

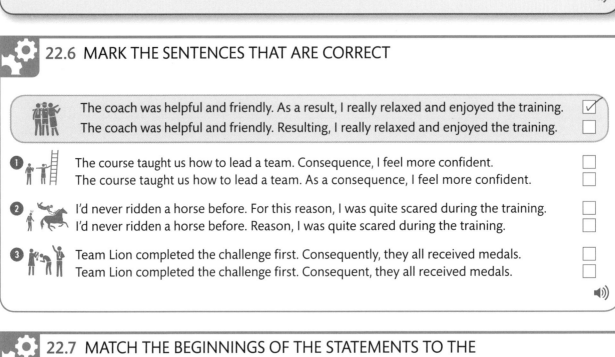

The coach was helpful and friendly. As a result, I really relaxed and enjoyed the training. ☑
The coach was helpful and friendly. Resulting, I really relaxed and enjoyed the training. ☐

❶ The course taught us how to lead a team. Consequence, I feel more confident. ☐
The course taught us how to lead a team. As a consequence, I feel more confident. ☐

❷ I'd never ridden a horse before. For this reason, I was quite scared during the training. ☐
I'd never ridden a horse before. Reason, I was quite scared during the training. ☐

❸ Team Lion completed the challenge first. Consequently, they all received medals. ☐
Team Lion completed the challenge first. Consequent, they all received medals. ☐

22.7 MATCH THE BEGINNINGS OF THE STATEMENTS TO THE CORRECT ENDINGS

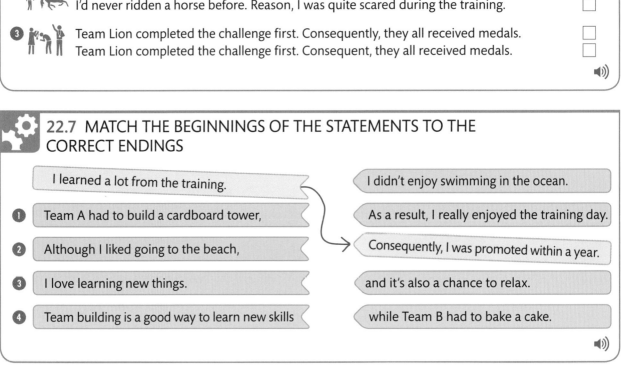

I learned a lot from the training.

❶ Team A had to build a cardboard tower,

❷ Although I liked going to the beach,

❸ I love learning new things.

❹ Team building is a good way to learn new skills

I didn't enjoy swimming in the ocean.

As a result, I really enjoyed the training day.

Consequently, I was promoted within a year.

and it's also a chance to relax.

while Team B had to bake a cake.

22.8 READ THE ARTICLE AND ANSWER THE QUESTIONS

94 MANAGEMENT TIPS

BUILDING A TEAM

CEO Lucia Gomez talks to us about team building

We send all our employees on team-building courses at least once a year. Our staff have gone on team-building treasure hunts, and they've also completed obstacle courses. However, what activity they do isn't so important. What matters is that they get out of the office and do something that requires them to communicate effectively, and support and help each other, too. It's quite easy to spot employees who are natural-born leaders during these activities. We sometimes identify future managers in this way and put them on our fast-track management-training program.

Activities are good for morale

Lucia's staff do team building every year.
True ☑ **False** ☐ **Not given** ☐

❶ Lucia's staff have learned how to sail.
True ☐ **False** ☐ **Not given** ☐

❷ Team building takes place away from work.
True ☐ **False** ☐ **Not given** ☐

❸ The choice of activity is very important.
True ☐ **False** ☐ **Not given** ☐

❹ During team building, staff work with new people.
True ☐ **False** ☐ **Not given** ☐

❺ Lucia can identify which employees are leaders.
True ☐ **False** ☐ **Not given** ☐

22.9 SAY THE SENTENCES OUT LOUD, CORRECTING THE ERRORS

This task is useful. It's however fun.

This task is useful. It's also fun.

❶ This course will teach you new skills. It will help you to get to know each other whereas.

❷ Equally Team B completed the task first, they had some major communication problems.

❸ By doing this task, we'll not only identify the team's weaknesses, but while its strengths.

❹ Team A worked together very well. Team B were whereas cooperative.

22 ✓ **CHECKLIST**

⚙ Discourse markers ☐   **Aa** Teamwork and team building ☐   🧩 Expressing your ideas ☐

23 Planning events

Many English verbs that are used to give opinions or talk about plans, intentions, and arrangements are followed by a gerund or an infinitive.

⚙ **New language** Verb patterns
Aa Vocabulary Corporate entertainment
🧩 **New skill** Talking about business events

23.1 KEY LANGUAGE VERBS AND GERUNDS / INFINITIVES

Some English verbs are followed by gerunds.

Verb ─→   ←─ Gerund

I really enjoy entertaining new clients at our company parties.

Other verbs, often those that express plans or intentions, are followed by an infinitive.

Verb ─→   ←─ Infinitive

Our clients expect to have high-quality accommodation.

23.2 HOW TO FORM VERBS AND GERUNDS / INFINITIVES

START OF SENTENCE	VERB	GERUND	REST OF SENTENCE
I really	enjoy	entertaining	new clients.

START OF SENTENCE	VERB	INFINITIVE	REST OF SENTENCE
Our clients	expect	to have	high-quality accommodation.

23.3 FURTHER EXAMPLES VERBS AND GERUNDS / INFINITIVES

 **I'll consider organizing the refreshments for our guests.**

 We must keep reminding clients of our product range.

 Sandeep has offered to welcome our visitors.

 We hope to impress our clients at the product launch.

23.4 CROSS OUT THE INCORRECT WORDS IN EACH SENTENCE

You need ~~being~~ / **to be** very organized to plan a successful business event.

① Mara has offered organizing / **to organize** the accommodation for our guests.

② I keep suggesting / **to suggest** that our company should organize a golf day, but my boss disagrees.

③ We like offering / **to offer** our clients a wide range of food at our conferences.

④ I enjoy helping / **to help** out at company open days because I get to meet lots of people.

⑤ Before I start planning, I usually make a list of all the customers I want inviting / **to invite**.

⑥ I expect staying / **to stay** late tonight to help Martina decorate the conference hall.

23.5 READ THE ADVERTISEMENT AND WRITE ANSWERS TO THE QUESTIONS AS FULL SENTENCES

TECHNOLOGY WEEKLY

Don't miss this year's SmartTech Fair!

Based in Tokyo, SmartTech Fair is one of the biggest IT fairs in the world. Established in 1987, each year's show is bigger and better than the last!

Don't miss out on these exciting seminars

CompuHealth seminar: Our industry expert examines how smart technology is helping us to live healthier lives.

Self-driving cars: Learn how these cutting-edge vehicles could shape the future of the car industry.

Register your interest online, and buy tickets in advance from the SmartTech website.

Which city is the SmartTech Fair in?
The SmartTech Fair is in Tokyo.

① What year did the SmartTech Fair open?

_____

② What is smart health technology helping to do?

_____

③ What could self-driving cars do?

_____

④ How can you show interest in attending an event?

_____

⑤ How can you buy tickets in advance?

_____

23.6 KEY LANGUAGE VERBS PLUS GERUND OR INFINITIVE (CHANGE IN MEANING)

Some verbs change their meaning depending
on the form of the verb that follows them.

**You remember meeting David, don't
you? He's the CEO of Unodom.**

[You have met David before. Do you remember?]

**You must remember to meet David to
make plans for the conference.**

[You must remember that you have to meet David.]

23.7 FURTHER EXAMPLES VERBS PLUS GERUND OR INFINITIVE (CHANGE IN MEANING)

In general, the gerund is often used for an action that happens before,
or at the same time as, that of the main verb. The infinitive is used to
describe an action that happens after the main verb's action.

VERB + GERUND	VERB + INFINITIVE

**I stopped reading the timetable
because my manager called me.**

[I was reading the timetable, but then I stopped.]

**I stopped to read the timetable
for our team training day.**

[I stopped what I was doing to read the timetable.]

**Sally went on talking all evening.
I hope you weren't bored.**

[Sally was talking for a long time.]

**Sally prepared her presentation, and went on
to talk about the company's new branding.**

[Sally gave the talk after she had prepared it.]

**I regret telling you that I can't come to dinner
with the clients. I can see that you're angry.**

[I wish I hadn't told you that I can't come to dinner.]

**I regret to tell you that I can't come to dinner
with the clients. I'm really sorry.**

[I'm sorry, but I can't come to dinner.]

23.8 MATCH THE BEGINNINGS OF THE SENTENCES TO THE CORRECT ENDINGS

I really regret making	to book the conference room.
1 We stopped holding breakfast meetings	until midnight in order to finish the report.
2 We regret to announce	that mistake at the conference.
3 I'm sure Shona will remember	that there will be some job losses.
4 Sahib went on working	because few people attended them.

23.9 LISTEN TO THE AUDIO AND ANSWER THE QUESTIONS

Sunita and Darren are arranging for some overseas clients to visit their office.

Two clients are visiting the office next week.
True ✓ **False** ☐ **Not given** ☐

1 Darren is not going to the meetings.
True ☐ **False** ☐ **Not given** ☐

2 The conference is about healthcare products.
True ☐ **False** ☐ **Not given** ☐

3 The conference is on Thursday.
True ☐ **False** ☐ **Not given** ☐

4 Sunita's boss expects her to impress the clients.
True ☐ **False** ☐ **Not given** ☐

5 It is Mr. Yamada's first visit to the US.
True ☐ **False** ☐ **Not given** ☐

6 They may go sightseeing with the clients.
True ☐ **False** ☐ **Not given** ☐

23.10 USE THE CHART TO CREATE NINE CORRECT SENTENCES AND SAY THEM OUT LOUD

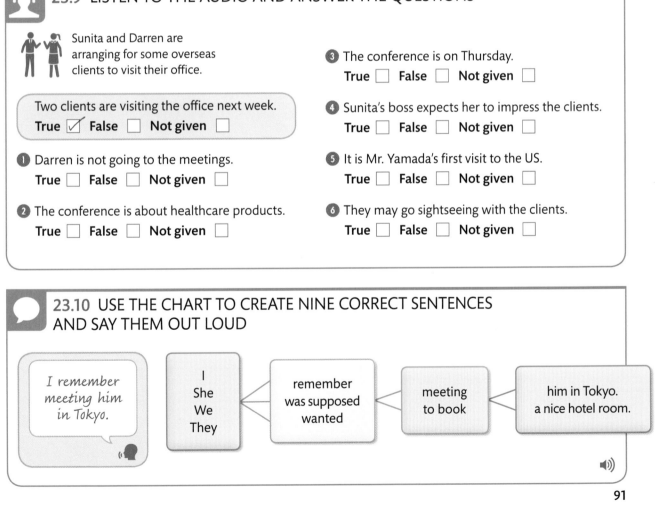

I remember meeting him in Tokyo.

| I / She / We / They | remember / was supposed / wanted | meeting / to book | him in Tokyo. / a nice hotel room. |

23.11 KEY LANGUAGE VERB + OBJECT + INFINITIVE

Some verbs, particularly ones that express orders or requests, can be followed by an object and another verb in the infinitive.

We expect all our staff **to attend** a party with our clients.

Verb — Object — Infinitive

23.12 HOW TO FORM VERB + OBJECT + INFINITIVE

SUBJECT	VERB	OBJECT	INFINITIVE	REST OF SENTENCE
We	expect	all our staff	to attend	a party with our clients.

23.13 FURTHER EXAMPLES VERB + OBJECT + INFINITIVE

I've invited our new clients to have lunch with us.

My manager asked me to book the conference room.

 ## 23.14 FILL IN THE GAPS USING THE PHRASES IN THE PANEL

We ___*want all our staff*___ to feel happy at work.

1. My boss asked me _____ a meeting with our clients.

2. Our clients _____ to visit them in Paris.

3. We expect all our staff _____ on time.

4. We _____ to attend our end-of-year party.

5. I expect my manager _____ me a promotion soon.

asked us

to arrange

to give

~~want all our staff~~

invited all our clients

to arrive

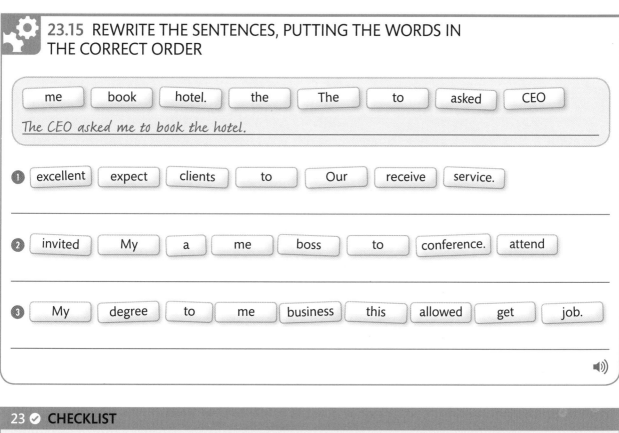

23.15 REWRITE THE SENTENCES, PUTTING THE WORDS IN THE CORRECT ORDER

| me | book | hotel. | the | The | to | asked | CEO |

The CEO asked me to book the hotel.

① | excellent | expect | clients | to | Our | receive | service. |

_____

② | invited | My | a | me | boss | to | conference. | attend |

_____

③ | My | degree | to | me | business | this | allowed | get | job. |

_____

23 ✓ CHECKLIST

⚙ Verb patterns ☐   Aa Corporate entertainment ☐   🧩 Talking about business events ☐

♻ REVIEW THE ENGLISH YOU HAVE LEARNED IN UNITS 19–23

NEW LANGUAGE	SAMPLE SENTENCE	☑	UNIT
GIVING ADVICE	You should ask the clients for more time. You must talk to your manager.	☐	19.1
MAKING SUGGESTIONS	What about hiring more staff? Why don't we open a new store?	☐	19.7
TALKING ABOUT ABILITIES	Jasmine's team can finish a job quickly. I couldn't give presentations five years ago.	☐	21.1, 21.5, 21.6
COMPARING AND CONTRASTING IDEAS	This task is useful. It is also fun. Team A won the task, whereas Team B lost.	☐	22.1, 22.2
VERBS WITH GERUNDS AND INFINITIVES	I really enjoy entertaining clients. Sandeep has offered to welcome our guests.	☐	23.1, 23.3, 23.6
VERB + OBJECT + INFINITIVE	We expect all our staff to attend the party.	☐	23.11

24 Vocabulary

24.1 MEETINGS

Lee, could you send out the agenda for Friday's meeting, please?

to send out an agenda
[to send a plan for what will be discussed]

The main objective of this meeting is to agree on a budget.

main objective
[the primary aim]

Yolanda is sick, so she will be absent from the meeting today.

to be absent
[to be not present]

Can we have a show of hands for those who agree with the proposal?

a show of hands
[a vote made by raising hands in the air to show agreement]

Francesca will give a presentation on health and safety.

to give a presentation
[to present information to a group of people]

Today we need to look at our sales figures for the last year.

to look at
[to consider or focus on something]

If we can't reach a consensus, we will have a vote.

to reach a consensus
[to come to an agreement about an issue]

We reached a unanimous agreement on the plan.

unanimous agreement
[when everyone agrees]

We will have another meeting next week because we have run out of time.

to run out of time
[to have no more time left to do something]

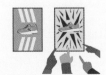

We will take questions at the end of the meeting.

to take questions
[to answer questions]

We need someone to take minutes during the meeting.

to take minutes
[to write a record of what was said during a meeting]

Did you manage to review the minutes from the last meeting?

to review the minutes
[to look again at the written record of a past meeting]

Please can you send the minutes to all attendees after the meeting?

attendees
[people who have been to or are going to a meeting]

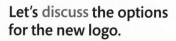

We need a strategy for increasing sales to young buyers.

a strategy
[a plan for achieving a particular goal]

Let's discuss the options for the new logo.

to discuss
[to talk about something]

I suggest that we use this new design.

to suggest / propose
[to put forward an idea or plan for others to discuss]

It's nearly lunchtime. Let's wrap up the meeting.

to wrap up
[to conclude or finish something]

I'm sorry to interrupt, but I have some more recent figures.

to interrupt
[to say something before someone else has finished speaking]

So to sum up, we really need to increase sales next month.

to sum up
[to conclude]

Excellent, we have three clear action points to work on.

action points
[proposals for specific action to be taken]

25 What people said

When telling co-workers what someone else said, you can take what they said (direct speech) and rephrase it accurately and clearly. This is called reported speech.

⚙ **New language** Reported speech
Aa Vocabulary Meetings
🧩 **New skill** Reporting what someone said

25.1 KEY LANGUAGE REPORTED SPEECH

The main verb in reported speech is usually "said." The reported verb is usually in a different tense from the direct speech.

Direct speech uses the present simple.

I can't come to the meeting. I'm too busy.

Luke said that he was too busy to come to the meeting.

"That" is usually added after "said" in reported speech.

Reported speech uses the past simple for the reported verb.

🔊

25.2 KEY LANGUAGE REPORTED SPEECH IN DIFFERENT TENSES

The tense used in reported speech is usually one tense back in time from the tense in direct speech.

I'm working in New York.

⬇

She said she was working in New York.
↳ Past continuous replaces present continuous.

I will call you soon.

⬇

He said he would call them soon.
↳ "Would" replaces "will."

I've been to China twice.

⬇

He said that he'd been to China twice.
↳ Past perfect replaces present perfect.

We can speak Japanese.

⬇

They said that they could speak Japanese.
↳ "Could" replaces "can."

🔊

25.3 KEY LANGUAGE REPORTED SPEECH AND THE PAST SIMPLE

The past simple in direct speech can either stay as the past simple or change to the past perfect in reported speech. The meaning is the same.

I arrived in Delhi on Saturday.

He said { he arrived / he'd arrived } in Delhi on Saturday.

25.4 MATCH THE DIRECT SPEECH TO THE REPORTED SPEECH

I'm working on the accounts. ──────────────▶ He said he was working on the accounts.

① I paid the invoice.

② I will pay the invoice.

③ I will arrange a meeting.

④ I'm arranging a meeting.

⑤ I've finished writing the report.

⑥ I'll finish writing the report.

She said she had finished writing the report.

He said he was arranging a meeting.

He said he would pay the invoice.

He said he would arrange a meeting.

She said she paid the invoice.

She said she would finish writing the report.

25.5 REWRITE THE SENTENCES, PUTTING THEM INTO REPORTED SPEECH

I need to send an email.
He _said that he needed to send an email._

① I will interview the candidates.
She _____

② I met the CEO on Monday.
He _____

③ I can book the meeting room.
He _____

④ I'm writing a press release.
She _____

⑤ I can use design software.
He _____

25.6 KEY LANGUAGE TIME AND PLACE REFERENCES

If speech is reported some time after it was said, words used to talk about times and places may need to change.

I went to work yesterday.

The time reference is "yesterday" in direct speech.

She said she'd been to work the day before.

The time reference is "the day before" in reported speech.

MAY 15 — MAY 16 — MAY 17

25.7 FURTHER EXAMPLES TIME AND PLACE REFERENCES

I'll call you tomorrow. → **He said he'd call me the following day.**

The weather is nice here. → **He told me the weather was nice there.**

We'll be closed this weekend. → **They said they'd be closed that weekend.**

I saw you last week. → **She said she'd seen me the week before.**

25.8 LISTEN TO THE AUDIO, THEN NUMBER THE REPORTED SENTENCES IN THE ORDER YOU HEAR THEM AS DIRECT SPEECH

Ⓐ Jack said he would send me the proposal the following day. ☐

Ⓑ Jack said he had got promoted the week before. ☐

Ⓒ Jack said he enjoyed working there. ☐

Ⓓ Jack said he'd be going to Dubai the following weekend. ☐ 1

Ⓔ Jack said he had gone to the London office the day before. ☐

25.9 KEY LANGUAGE OTHER CHANGES IN REPORTED SPEECH

In reported speech, pronouns may also need to be changed
to ensure they refer to the correct person or thing.

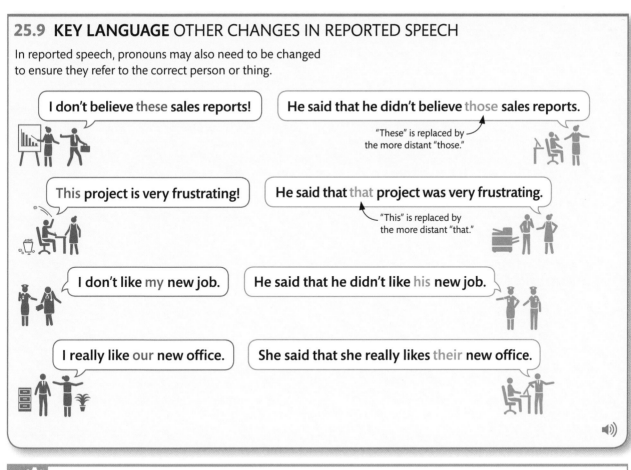

I don't believe **these** sales reports!

He said that he didn't believe **those** sales reports.

"These" is replaced by
the more distant "those."

This project is very frustrating!

He said that **that** project was very frustrating.

"This" is replaced by
the more distant "that."

I don't like **my** new job.

He said that he didn't like **his** new job.

I really like **our** new office.

She said that she really likes **their** new office.

25.10 REWRITE THE SENTENCES, PUTTING THE WORDS IN THE CORRECT ORDER

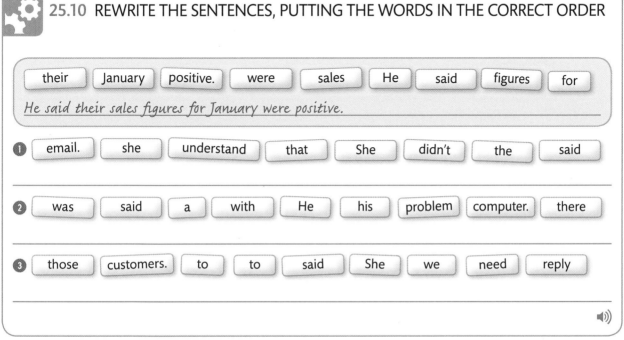

| their | January | positive. | were | sales | He | said | figures | for |

He said their sales figures for January were positive.

1. | email. | she | understand | that | She | didn't | the | said |

2. | was | said | a | with | He | his | problem | computer. | there |

3. | those | customers. | to | to | said | She | we | need | reply |

25.11 KEY LANGUAGE "TELL" IN REPORTED SPEECH

In reported speech, "tell" can also be used as the main verb. It must be followed by an object, which shows who someone is talking to.

I have to change the meeting date.

He told me that he had to change the meeting date.

Unlike "say," "tell" must be followed by an object.

25.12 KEY LANGUAGE REPORTING VERBS WITH "THAT"

"Say" and "tell" do not give any information about the speaker's manner. They can be replaced with other verbs that suggest the speaker's mood or reason for speaking.

I'm not very good at sales.

Neil admitted that he wasn't very good at sales.

"Admit" suggests a confession on the part of the speaker.

25.13 FURTHER EXAMPLES REPORTING VERBS WITH "THAT"

We have to close the building for security tests.

They explained that the building had to be closed for security tests.

Your office is huge! It has a nice view, too.

Rohit admired our office, and added that it had a nice view.

That's right! Our profits have risen this year.

Jeremy confirmed that our profits had risen this year.

25.14 REPORT THE DIRECT SPEECH IN THE AUDIO OUT LOUD, FILLING IN THE GAPS USING THE WORDS IN THE PANEL

I am not the person in charge of this project.

He _____*denied*_____ that he was the person in charge of that project.

1. Yes, that's right. The sales figures will be ready by 5pm.

Sharon _____ that the sales figures would be ready by 5pm.

2. Don't worry. I'll definitely stay late to help you finish the report.

Lilia _____ that she would stay late to help me finish the report.

3. We have beaten our sales target for the year.

Mr. Lee _____ that we had beaten our sales target for the year.

4. The coffee from the machine tastes awful.

Ben _____ that the coffee from the machine tasted awful.

5. Perhaps you could ask your boss about a raise.

She _____ that I could ask my boss about a raise.

complained   announced   confirmed   suggested   ~~denied~~   promised

26 What people asked

You can use reported questions to tell someone what someone else has asked. Direct questions and reported questions have different word orders.

⚙ **New language** Reported questions
Aa **Vocabulary** "Have," "make," "get," "do"
🧩 **New skill** Reporting what someone asked

26.1 KEY LANGUAGE REPORTED OPEN QUESTIONS

Direct open questions are reported by swapping the order of the subject and the verb, and changing the tense of the verb.

Where is my laptop?

Adam asked me where his laptop was. **Have you seen it?**

26.2 HOW TO FORM REPORTED OPEN QUESTIONS

SUBJECT	REPORTING VERB	OBJECT	QUESTION WORD	SUBJECT	VERB
Adam	**asked**	**me**	**where**	**his laptop**	**was.**

The main verb in reported questions is usually "ask."

The object can be left out.

The subject comes before the verb in reported questions.

The tense moves one tense back from direct speech.

26.3 FURTHER EXAMPLES REPORTED OPEN QUESTIONS

Why can't you **come to the meeting?**

He asked me why I couldn't **come to the meeting.**

An object can be included to say who was asked the original question.

What do you think **about the suggestions?**

They asked me what I thought **about the suggestions.**

When a question uses the verb "do," this is left out of reported questions.

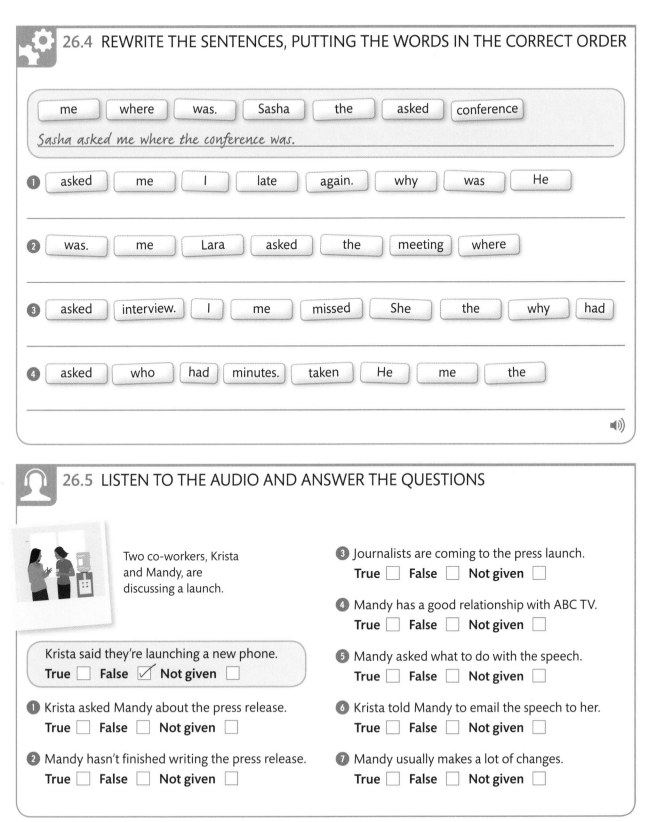

26.4 REWRITE THE SENTENCES, PUTTING THE WORDS IN THE CORRECT ORDER

| me | where | was. | Sasha | the | asked | conference |

Sasha asked me where the conference was.

1 | asked | me | I | late | again. | why | was | He |

_____

2 | was. | me | Lara | asked | the | meeting | where |

_____

3 | asked | interview. | I | me | missed | She | the | why | had |

_____

4 | asked | who | had | minutes. | taken | He | me | the |

_____

26.5 LISTEN TO THE AUDIO AND ANSWER THE QUESTIONS

Two co-workers, Krista and Mandy, are discussing a launch.

Krista said they're launching a new phone.
True ☐ **False** ☐ **Not given** ☑

1 Krista asked Mandy about the press release.
True ☐ **False** ☐ **Not given** ☐

2 Mandy hasn't finished writing the press release.
True ☐ **False** ☐ **Not given** ☐

3 Journalists are coming to the press launch.
True ☐ **False** ☐ **Not given** ☐

4 Mandy has a good relationship with ABC TV.
True ☐ **False** ☐ **Not given** ☐

5 Mandy asked what to do with the speech.
True ☐ **False** ☐ **Not given** ☐

6 Krista told Mandy to email the speech to her.
True ☐ **False** ☐ **Not given** ☐

7 Mandy usually makes a lot of changes.
True ☐ **False** ☐ **Not given** ☐

26.6 READ THE ARTICLE AND ANSWER THE QUESTIONS

You must have meetings in order to do business.
True ☐ **False** ☐ **Not given** ☑

1 You should limit the number of things to discuss.
True ☐ **False** ☐ **Not given** ☐

2 There is no need to share the agenda.
True ☐ **False** ☐ **Not given** ☐

3 Let attendees know how long the lunch break is.
True ☐ **False** ☐ **Not given** ☐

4 People tend to take a long break after a meeting.
True ☐ **False** ☐ **Not given** ☐

5 People rarely forget to organize the meeting location.
True ☐ **False** ☐ **Not given** ☐

6 A good meeting room has plenty of light.
True ☐ **False** ☐ **Not given** ☐

BUSINESS TIPS

Preparation is key

CEO David Moss explains how to have successful meetings

It is important to decide your main objectives before the meeting. Create an agenda and send it to all attendees so they can prepare in advance. Set a date and time for your meeting. Decide when you will have a break, and how long you will give attendees to have lunch. If you don't do this, people might take long breaks, reducing your meeting time! Last of all, this sounds simple, but it's easy to forget to make arrangements for the meeting location, especially if you're very busy. Get the room ready with the right amount of chairs and refreshments, and your laptop or any other necessary equipment.

Aa 26.7 FILL IN THE GAPS USING THE WORDS IN THE PANEL TO CREATE MORE COLLOCATIONS WITH "HAVE," "MAKE," "GET," AND "DO"

Suzi suggested that in a couple of years, I could [get _a job_] in the Paris office.

1 The boss is angry with Max. He told him to [do] before he leaves.

2 Mr. Tan promised that I would [get] to manager if I worked hard.

3 Could you [do] ? Could you make 20 copies of this, please?

4 Can I [make] ? Finish the proposal first, then work on the spreadsheet.

5 Paola said that she usually [gets] from work at 6:30pm.

6 Paul said that he [had] with his boss, but he was really late.

his work   a suggestion   ~~a job~~   me a favor   an appointment   home   promoted

26.8 KEY LANGUAGE REPORTED CLOSED QUESTIONS

If the answer to a question is "yes" or "no," "if" or "whether" is used to report the question.

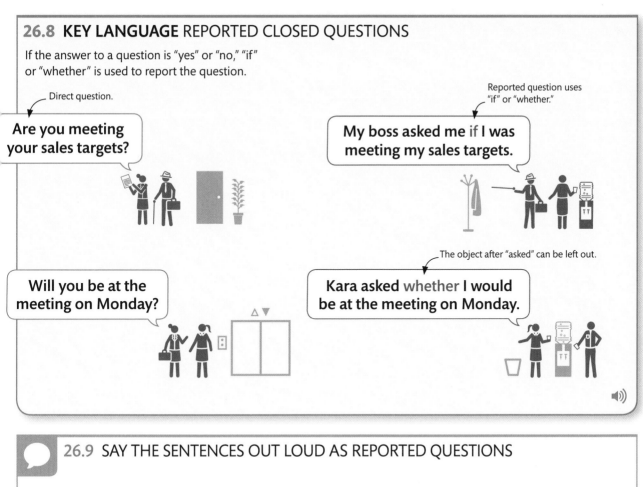

Direct question.

Are you meeting your sales targets?

Reported question uses "if" or "whether."

My boss asked me if I was meeting my sales targets.

Will you be at the meeting on Monday?

The object after "asked" can be left out.

Kara asked whether I would be at the meeting on Monday.

26.9 SAY THE SENTENCES OUT LOUD AS REPORTED QUESTIONS

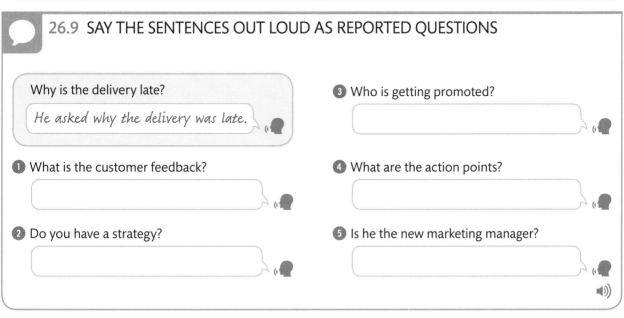

Why is the delivery late?

He asked why the delivery was late.

❶ What is the customer feedback?

❷ Do you have a strategy?

❸ Who is getting promoted?

❹ What are the action points?

❺ Is he the new marketing manager?

27 Reporting quantities

In presentations and reports, you may need to talk about how much of something there is. The words you can use to do this depend on the thing you are describing.

🔧 **New language** "Few," "little," and "all"
Aa Vocabulary Meetings
🧩 **New skill** Talking about quantity

27.1 KEY LANGUAGE "FEW" FOR SMALL NUMBERS

"Few" is used with plural countable nouns to say that there are not many of something. It emphasizes how small the number is.

> few = not many

 There have been few new customers this quarter.

"Few" can also be used as a pronoun to mean "not many."

 So few are willing to spend money for the deluxe range.

"A few" is used with countable nouns to mean "some." It emphasizes that the number, though small, is enough.

> a few = some

 I have a few suggestions for how to improve sales.

"Very" can be used to stress that the number of something is even smaller.

 We have very few items left in stock.

🔊

27.2 MARK THE SENTENCES THAT ARE CORRECT

You'll be glad to hear that we still have a few options available to us this year. ☑
You'll be glad to hear that we still have few options available to us this year. ☐

1. We'll have to reduce the price. A few customers have bought our new jeans. ☐
   We'll have to reduce the price. Very few customers have bought our new jeans. ☐

2. So few people pay by check these days that we no longer accept this form of payment. ☐
   A few people pay by check these days that we no longer accept this form of payment. ☐

3. Unfortunately, we've had a few inquiries about our new spa treatments. ☐
   Unfortunately, we've had few inquiries about our new spa treatments. ☐

🔊

27.3 KEY LANGUAGE "LITTLE" FOR SMALL AMOUNTS

"Little" is used with uncountable nouns to say that there is not much of something in UK English. It emphasizes how small the amount is.

"A little" is used with uncountable nouns to mean "some." It emphasizes that the amount, though small, is enough.

little = not much

I have little doubt that next year will be challenging.

a little = some

The summer should offer a little boost to sales.

"Little" can also be used as a pronoun to mean "not much."

Very little can be done to improve the short-term performance.

Informally, "a (little) bit of" can be used instead of "a little."

There's a little bit of time left to discuss our options.

27.4 CROSS OUT THE INCORRECT WORD IN EACH SENTENCE, THEN SAY THE SENTENCES OUT LOUD

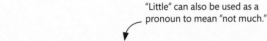

I'm afraid that there are ~~little~~ / few options left for us to explore.

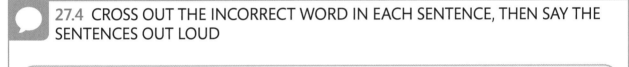

❶ Unfortunately, there is a little / little chance of us winning this contract.

❷ I have a few / few ideas that I really think could improve our brand image.

❸ There is still a little / a few time left before we need to submit the report.

❹ Kelvin has little / few understanding of accountancy.

❺ So few / a few people have bought this TV that we're going to stop production.

27.5 KEY LANGUAGE "ALL" AS A PRONOUN

"All" can sometimes be used as a pronoun to mean either "everything" or "the only thing."

all = everything	all = the only thing

 I hope all goes well in the presentation.

 All we can do is hope that they like the product.

 ## 27.6 REWRITE THE SENTENCES, PUTTING THE WORDS IN THE CORRECT ORDER

about	told	all	you	I	know	have	it.	I

I have told you all I know about it.

1 | do | can | is | your | mistake. | apologize | All | for | you |

2 | expect | I | is | tasks. | to | All | complete | for | staff | their |

3 | sure | be | the | I'm | will | interview. | well | in | all |

4 | I | is | All | raise. | want | a |

5 | all | have | information | We | the | need. | we |

27.7 MATCH THE PAIRS OF SENTENCES THAT MEAN THE SAME THING

There's little money left in the budget.

1. All we need is a photo of the product.
2. There's a little bit of money left.
3. There's a little time left.
4. Few staff members like Mr. Jenkins.
5. Bertha knows all there is to know about IT.
6. A few staff members like Mr. Jenkins.
7. There's little time left.

We have some time.

Not many people like Mr. Jenkins.

We don't have much money.

We don't have much time.

Some people like Mr. Jenkins.

The only thing we need is a photo.

Bertha is an expert in IT.

We have some money.

27.8 LISTEN TO THE AUDIO AND ANSWER THE QUESTIONS

A sales executive is reporting to his manager about the results from the last quarter.

There are very few dog toys left.
True ✓ **False** ☐ **Not given** ☐

1. The Woof Doggy toy is a new product.
True ☐ **False** ☐ **Not given** ☐

2. It'll be easy to get the supplier to deliver more toys.
True ☐ **False** ☐ **Not given** ☐

3. The boss suggests asking for part of an order.
True ☐ **False** ☐ **Not given** ☐

4. There are no princess costumes left.
True ☐ **False** ☐ **Not given** ☐

5. The princess dress will be delivered next quarter.
True ☐ **False** ☐ **Not given** ☐

6. The camping kit has been very popular.
True ☐ **False** ☐ **Not given** ☐

27 ✓ **CHECKLIST**

⚙ "Few," "little," and "all" ☐   **Aa** Meetings ☐   🧩 Talking about quantity ☐

28 Checking information

Sometimes you may need to clarify whether you have understood a point. There are a number of ways to politely check information in conversation.

🔧 **New language** Subject questions, question tags
Aa Vocabulary Polite checks and echo questions
🧩 **New skill** Checking information

28.1 KEY LANGUAGE SUBJECT QUESTIONS

In English, most questions ask about the person or thing receiving that action (the object). If you want to find out or confirm who or what did an action, you can use subject questions.

Question doesn't use "did."

Who took the minutes?

The answer is the subject of the question.

Miranda took the minutes.

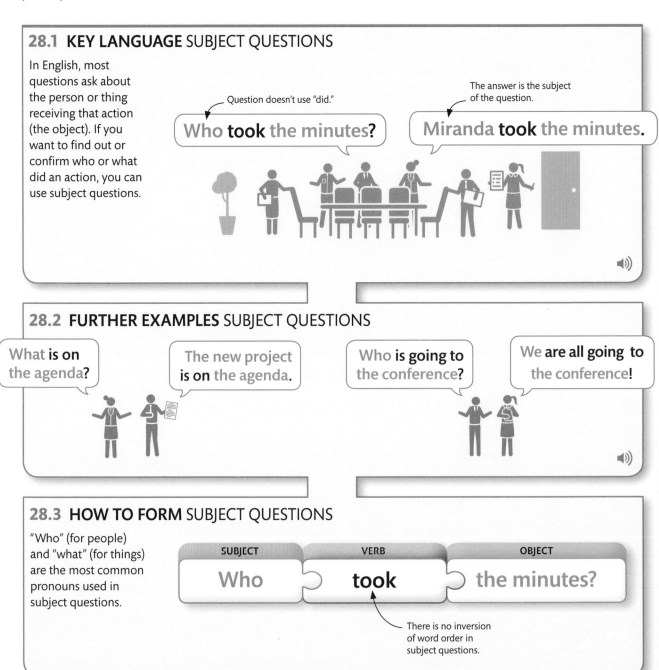

28.2 FURTHER EXAMPLES SUBJECT QUESTIONS

What is on the agenda?

The new project is on the agenda.

Who is going to the conference?

We are all going to the conference!

28.3 HOW TO FORM SUBJECT QUESTIONS

"Who" (for people) and "what" (for things) are the most common pronouns used in subject questions.

SUBJECT	VERB	OBJECT
Who	took	the minutes?

There is no inversion of word order in subject questions.

28.4 REWRITE THE QUESTIONS, PUTTING THE WORDS IN THE CORRECT ORDER

the | is | problem? | What

What is the problem?

1. manager? | Who | the | is

_____

2. the | What's | in | report?

_____

3. answers | telephone? | Who | the

_____

4. approves | Who | annual | vacation?

_____

5. is | What | deadline? | the

_____

6. wrote | the | ad? | Who

_____

7. take | Who | questions? | will

_____

8. are | the | What | objectives?

_____

9. the | What's | about? | complaint

_____

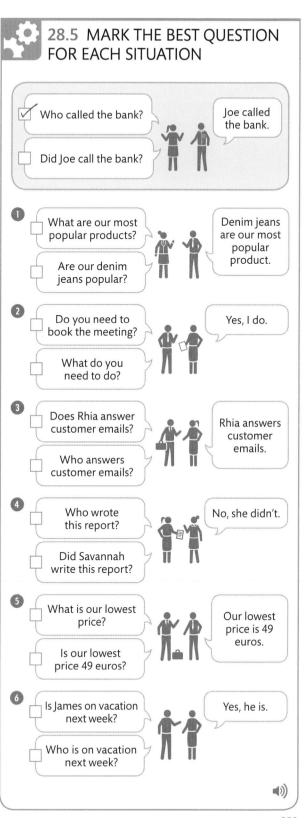

28.5 MARK THE BEST QUESTION FOR EACH SITUATION

☑ Who called the bank?

☐ Did Joe call the bank?

Joe called the bank.

1. ☐ What are our most popular products?

☐ Are our denim jeans popular?

Denim jeans are our most popular product.

2. ☐ Do you need to book the meeting?

☐ What do you need to do?

Yes, I do.

3. ☐ Does Rhia answer customer emails?

☐ Who answers customer emails?

Rhia answers customer emails.

4. ☐ Who wrote this report?

☐ Did Savannah write this report?

No, she didn't.

5. ☐ What is our lowest price?

☐ Is our lowest price 49 euros?

Our lowest price is 49 euros.

6. ☐ Is James on vacation next week?

☐ Who is on vacation next week?

Yes, he is.

28.6 KEY LANGUAGE QUESTION TAGS

Another way to check information is by using question tags. The simplest question tags use the verb "be" with a pronoun matching the subject of the sentence.

STATEMENT **QUESTION TAG**

Hi everyone! I'm late, aren't I?

For statements with "I," "aren't I?" is used in the negative question tag, not "amn't I?"

For most verbs other than "be," a present simple statement is followed by a question tag with "do" or "does."

PRESENT SIMPLE **QUESTION TAG**

Jack takes the calls, doesn't he?

A past simple statement is followed by a question tag with "did."

PAST SIMPLE **QUESTION TAG**

Susan studied accounting, didn't she?

A statement with an auxiliary verb is followed by a question tag with the same auxiliary.

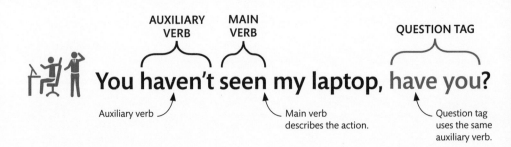

AUXILIARY VERB **MAIN VERB** **QUESTION TAG**

You haven't seen my laptop, have you?

Auxiliary verb

Main verb describes the action.

Question tag uses the same auxiliary verb.

Statements with modal verbs such as "could," "would," and "should" are followed by question tags with the same modal.

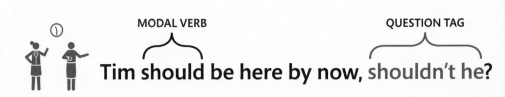

MODAL VERB **QUESTION TAG**

Tim should be here by now, shouldn't he?

28.7 HOW TO FORM QUESTION TAGS

A positive statement is followed by a negative question tag,
and a negative statement is followed by a positive question tag.

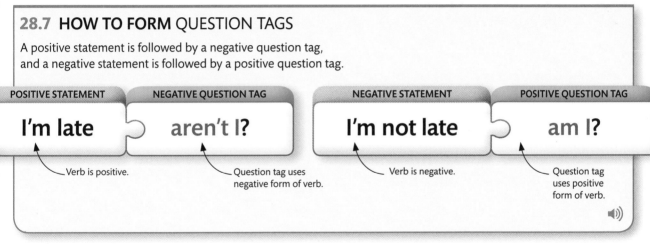

POSITIVE STATEMENT	NEGATIVE QUESTION TAG	NEGATIVE STATEMENT	POSITIVE QUESTION TAG
I'm late	**aren't I?**	**I'm not late**	**am I?**

Verb is positive.

Question tag uses negative form of verb.

Verb is negative.

Question tag uses positive form of verb.

28.8 MATCH THE BEGINNINGS OF THE SENTENCES TO THE CORRECT QUESTION TAGS

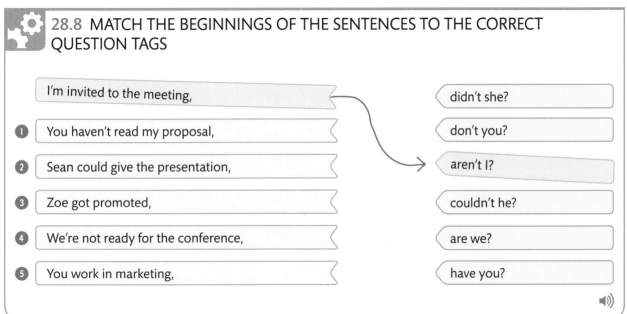

I'm invited to the meeting, —————→ aren't I?

didn't she?

don't you?

① You haven't read my proposal,

② Sean could give the presentation,

couldn't he?

③ Zoe got promoted,

are we?

④ We're not ready for the conference,

have you?

⑤ You work in marketing,

28.9 FILL IN THE GAPS USING THE CORRECT QUESTION TAGS

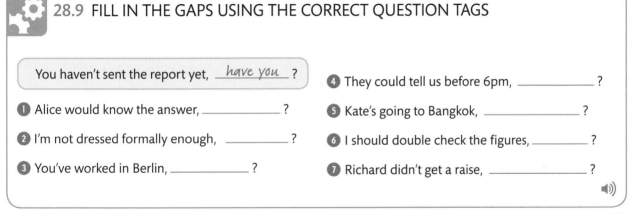

You haven't sent the report yet, _*have you*_ ?

① Alice would know the answer, _____ ?

② I'm not dressed formally enough, _____ ?

③ You've worked in Berlin, _____ ?

④ They could tell us before 6pm, _____ ?

⑤ Kate's going to Bangkok, _____ ?

⑥ I should double check the figures, _____ ?

⑦ Richard didn't get a raise, _____ ?

28.10 VOCABULARY POLITE CHECKS AND ECHO QUESTIONS

There are also certain set phrases you can use to politely check information.

Pardon?

Could you say that again? I didn't catch it.

What was the last figure? I didn't hear it.

Sorry, I missed that.

Be careful not to say "What?" too directly, as it can sound rude.

You can also repeat the important word or phrase you want to check, or echo part or all of the sentence with a question word or phrase at the end.

We sold $40,000 of stock to Japan last month.

To Japan?

We sold $40,000 of stock to where?

28.11 LISTEN TO THE AUDIO AND ANSWER THE QUESTIONS

A sales assistant is calling her manager to check a few details and confirm information.

The standard discount offered is 30%.
True ☐ **False** ☐ **Not given** ☑

1 Discounts are offered to long-term customers.
True ☐ **False** ☐ **Not given** ☐

2 If a customer buys 1,000 units, they get 15% off.
True ☐ **False** ☐ **Not given** ☐

3 A new customer in Thailand sent an inquiry.
True ☐ **False** ☐ **Not given** ☐

4 They already work with companies in Asia.
True ☐ **False** ☐ **Not given** ☐

5 Julian will find out more about the new customer.
True ☐ **False** ☐ **Not given** ☐

28.12 CROSS OUT THE INCORRECT WORDS IN EACH SENTENCE, THEN SAY THE SENTENCES OUT LOUD

We've made good progress, haven't / ~~have~~ we?

1. What was the name of the company? I didn't listen / hear.

2. Who / What is working on the project for the new office?

3. You identified the mistake, haven't you / didn't you?

4. Could you repeat that, please? I didn't catch / grab it.

5. Where / What is the theme of this year's conference?

---

28 ✓ CHECKLIST

⚙ Subject questions, question tags ☐   **Aa** Polite checks and echo questions ☐   🧩 Checking information ☐

♺ REVIEW THE ENGLISH YOU HAVE LEARNED IN UNITS 24–28

NEW LANGUAGE	SAMPLE SENTENCE	☑	UNIT
REPORTED SPEECH	Luke said that he felt sick. She said she'd been to work the day before.	☐	25.1, 25.6, 25.9
REPORTING VERBS	Jeremy confirmed that our profits had risen.	☐	25.12
REPORTED QUESTIONS	Adam asked me where his laptop was.	☐	26.1, 26.8
"FEW," "LITTLE," AND "ALL"	I have a few suggestions. Very little can be done. I hope all goes well.	☐	27.1, 27.3, 27.5
CHECKING INFORMATION WITH SUBJECT QUESTIONS AND QUESTION TAGS	Who took the minutes? I'm late, aren't I?	☐	28.1, 28.6
POLITE CHECKS AND ECHO QUESTIONS	Sorry, I missed that. We sold $40,000 of stock to where?	☐	28.10

Aa 29.1 INDUSTRIES

education

healthcare

catering / food

chemical

construction

agriculture / farming

energy

electronics

entertainment

fashion

finance

fishing

hospitality

journalism

manufacturing

advertising

mining

petroleum

pharmaceutical

real estate (US) / property (UK)

recycling

shipping

tourism

transportation

29.2 PROFESSIONAL ATTRIBUTES

accurate

adaptable

ambitious

calm

confident

creative

customer-focused

determined

efficient

energetic

flexible

hardworking

honest

independent

innovative

motivated

organized

patient

practical

professional

punctual

reliable

responsible

team player

30 Job descriptions

English uses "a" or "an" in descriptions of jobs and to introduce new information. The zero article refers to general things, and "the" refers to specific things.

⚙ **New language** Articles
Aa Vocabulary Job descriptions and applications
New skill Describing a job

30.1 KEY LANGUAGE "A" AND "AN"

Use "a" or "an" to introduce new information. Use "the" when the reader or listener already knows what you are talking about.

Use "a" because this is the first time "job" is mentioned.

Use "an" before a vowel sound.

I applied for a job last week as an engineer.
The application form was really long.

Use "the" because it is clear from the context that this is the application form for the engineer job.

🔊

30.2 CROSS OUT THE INCORRECT WORDS IN EACH SENTENCE

A / An / The salary for this job is really good.

1 A / An / The deadline for applications is Friday.

2 This job is based in a / an / the Berlin office.

3 We are recruiting a / an / the new designer.

4 I've got a / an / the interview for a new job.

5 A / An / The application form for this job is long.

6 Please complete a / an / the form on our website.

7 A / An / The ideal candidate enjoys teamwork.

8 There's an ad for a / an / the English teacher.

🔊

30.3 LISTEN TO THE AUDIO, THEN NUMBER THE PICTURES IN THE ORDER THEY ARE DESCRIBED

30.4 KEY LANGUAGE ZERO AND DEFINITE ARTICLES (PLURALS)

With plurals, English uses no article (zero article) to talk about things in general. Use "the" (definite article) to talk about specific things.

General

Catering jobs are very well paid at the moment.

Specific

The catering jobs at this café are really well paid.

30.5 FURTHER EXAMPLES ZERO AND DEFINITE ARTICLES (PLURALS)

Accountants have to work very hard.
The accountants at my office work long hours.

Managers don't always listen to their staff.
The managers here can't run a team.

Noriko loves giving presentations.
The presentations she gave last week were great.

30.6 MARK THE SENTENCES THAT ARE CORRECT

Most doctors have to work long hours. They are very dedicated people. ☑
Most the doctors have to work long hours. They are the very dedicated people. ☐

1. The jobs I'm really interested in are based in Los Angeles. They're in IT. ☐
   Jobs I'm really interested in are based in Los Angeles. They're in the IT. ☐

2. People who interviewed me for the job were really nice. They were managers. ☐
   The people who interviewed me for the job were really nice. They were the managers. ☐

3. Clients can be very demanding. The clients I met today had lots of complaints. ☐
   The clients can be very demanding. Clients I met today had lots of the complaints. ☐

30.7 KEY LANGUAGE MORE USES OF THE ZERO ARTICLE

Use the zero article to talk about company names, place names
(including most countries and continents), and languages.

Apollo AV is looking to recruit an International Marketing Manager.

The successful candidate must speak excellent French **and** Italian.

The role involves travel to France **and all over** Europe.

30.8 KEY LANGUAGE MORE USES OF THE DEFINITE ARTICLE

Use "the" to talk about specific roles and departments
within a company, and for international organizations.

I applied for a job in the finance department **at your company.**

I have an interview with the Head of HR **and** the CEO.

The United Nations is recruiting a scientific researcher.

30.9 REWRITE THE SENTENCES, CORRECTING THE ERRORS

She works in design department.
She works in the design department.

❶ I often travel to the Hong Kong on business.

❷ The Zenith Accounting has three job openings.

❸ I have a meeting with company director.

❹ He works for World Health Organization.

❺ I'm a strong candidate because I speak the Russian.

30.10 REWRITE THE HIGHLIGHTED PHRASES, CORRECTING THE ERRORS

FLIGHT ATTENDANT

The Golden Wings Ltd. is hiring! Our airline flies throughout the Europe and Asia, and we have a opening for a bright, enthusiastic flight attendant. Have you go what it takes? A Flight attendants must be polite, hard-working and presentable. If this sounds like you, then we'd love to hear from you. An hours can be long, but the job is well paid, and you will have the

chance to stay in the best hotels and locations across the world. This is a once-in-a-lifetime opportunity to see the world and build the career. Apply now!

Golden Wings Ltd.

1 _____
2 _____
3 _____
4 _____
5 _____

30.11 CROSS OUT THE INCORRECT WORDS IN EACH SENTENCE, THEN SAY THE SENTENCES OUT LOUD

~~Salary in this job~~ / The salary in this job is really good.

1 Your meeting is with HR manager / the HR manager.

2 We're recruiting more staff in France / the France.

3 I'm looking for a job as education consultant / an education consultant.

4 We need someone who can speak the Italian / Italian.

5 Omnitech / The Omnitech is advertising several vacancies in its marketing department.

6 I work in sales department / the sales department of a large company.

---

30 ✓ CHECKLIST

⚙ Articles ☐   Aa Job descriptions and applications ☐   🧩 Describing a job ☐

31 Applying for a job

Cover letters for job applications should sound fluent and confident. Using the correct prepositions after verbs, nouns, and adjectives can help you achieve this.

New language Dependent prepositions
Aa Vocabulary Cover-letter vocabulary
New skill Writing a cover letter

31.1 KEY LANGUAGE DEPENDENT PREPOSITIONS

Some English words cannot be used on their own. They need to be followed by specific "dependent" prepositions.

"Apply" cannot be paired with any other preposition in this context.

I am writing to apply for the position of Senior Police Officer.

31.2 FURTHER EXAMPLES DEPENDENT PREPOSITIONS

I graduated from college in June 2015.

He is highly trained in all aspects of catering.

At college, I focused on mechanical engineering.

As Deputy Director, I reported to the CEO.

31.3 CROSS OUT THE INCORRECT WORDS IN EACH SENTENCE

In my role as Senior Production Manager, I reported in̶ / b̶y̶ / to the Production Director.

1. In our department, we focus at / **on** / to sales and marketing.

2. Katrina graduated at / in / **from** college with a degree in Biological Sciences.

3. Our technicians are fully trained to / with / **in** all aspects of health and safety.

4. I've applied at / to / **for** a job in the IT department of a big company in Los Angeles.

31.4 READ THE COVER LETTER AND ANSWER THE QUESTIONS

Sasha heard about the job on the radio.
True ☐   False ☑   Not given ☐

1 Sasha is currently a senior travel executive.
True ☐   False ☐   Not given ☐

2 She has worked for the same company for 10 years.
True ☐   False ☐   Not given ☐

3 She is responsible for travel to Southeast Asia.
True ☐   False ☐   Not given ☐

4 She is tired of working in the travel industry.
True ☐   False ☐   Not given ☐

5 She would like to learn new skills.
True ☐   False ☐   Not given ☐

6 She has provided written recommendations with her application.
True ☐   False ☐   Not given ☐

Dear Mr. Goméz,

I am writing to apply for the position of Senior Travel Representative, as advertised in Go Travel! magazine.

I have worked in the travel industry for more than 10 years, and have experience handling both package vacations and tailor-made trips. In my current position, I am responsible for travel to Southeast Asia, and last year I was responsible for more than 15,000 customers. My sales figures amounted to more than $12 million.

I am passionate about working in the travel industry and would welcome the opportunity to learn new skills and broaden my experience. I'm extremely reliable and hard-working.

Please find attached my résumé and references. I look forward to hearing from you.

Yours sincerely,

Sasha Mailovitch

31.5 MATCH THE PHRASES THAT MEAN THE SAME

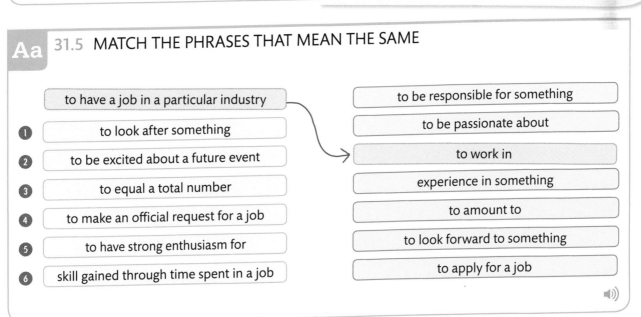

to have a job in a particular industry

1 to look after something
2 to be excited about a future event
3 to equal a total number
4 to make an official request for a job
5 to have strong enthusiasm for
6 skill gained through time spent in a job

to be responsible for something
to be passionate about
to work in
experience in something
to amount to
to look forward to something
to apply for a job

31.6 KEY LANGUAGE DEPENDENT PREPOSITIONS (CHANGE IN MEANING)

Some words can be paired with different dependent prepositions.
Their meaning changes depending on which preposition is used.

**I worked with the head chef
in a busy restaurant.**

[The head chef was a colleague.]

**I worked for the head chef
in a busy restaurant.**

[The head chef was my boss.]

31.7 FURTHER EXAMPLES DEPENDENT PREPOSITIONS (CHANGE IN MEANING)

I heard about the job on your website.

[I heard that the job was open.]

I look forward to hearing from you.

[I look forward to you responding to me.]

I was responsible for a rise in sales.

[I was responsible for sales going up.]

Last year, there was a rise of 40 percent.

[Sales went up by 40 percent.]

31.8 FILL IN THE GAPS WITH THE CORRECT PREPOSITION

Jake and I are both trainee hairdressers. I have been working ___*with*___ him for two months.

❶ When can I expect to hear _____ you about the job?

❷ Unfortunately, there has been a rise _____ complaints from customers.

❸ I work _____ the CEO of a big IT company. I'm her assistant.

❹ I heard _____ the job through a friend who works at the company.

❺ Our profits went up last year. There was a rise _____ about five percent.

124

Aa 31.9 USING THE CLUES, WRITE THE WORDS FROM THE PANEL IN THE CORRECT PLACES ON THE GRID

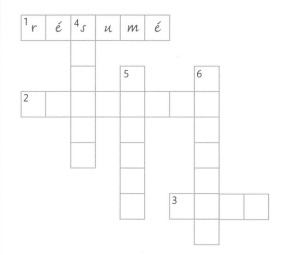

ACROSS

1 A document detailing your qualifications

2 Honest and trustworthy

3 The group of people you work with

DOWN

4 A set of abilities resulting from experience

5 A fixed regular payment

6 A person who gives a formal recommendation

skills   salary   ~~résumé~~

team   referee   reliable

31.10 READ THE COVER LETTER AND CROSS OUT THE INCORRECT WORDS

64 Elm Tree Way
West Clinton
PO13 4JS

Dear Mr. Khan,
I am writing to apply for / apply with the position / positioning of head web designer with your company.

I have experience at / experience in managing large commercial websites. Last year, sales from the website that I designed for a major online store amounted at / amounted to more than $6 million.

I am eager to develop my skilful / skills and broaden my knowledge of other industries / industrial.
I believe this job would be a fantastic opponent / opportunity for me, and I'd add a great deal to your company. I am enthusiastic and passionate for / passionate about being at the cutting edge of web development. I'm also very reliability / reliable and I enjoy working in a team.

I have attached my résumé / cover letter and details of my referees. I look forward to hearing to / hearing from you.

Yours sincerely,
Amy Quah

32 Job interviews

In a job interview, it is important to describe your achievements in a specific and detailed way. You can use relative clauses to do this.

⚙ **New language** Relative clauses
Aa Vocabulary Job interviews
🧩 **New skill** Describing your achievements in detail

32.1 KEY LANGUAGE DEFINING RELATIVE CLAUSES

Defining relative clauses give essential information that helps to identify a person or thing. Here, the defining relative clause gives essential information about a thing.

> Could you tell me more about yourself?

MAIN CLAUSE / DEFINING RELATIVE CLAUSE

This is the product that I designed last year.

In defining relative clauses, this is the relative pronoun for things.

Here, the defining relative clause gives essential information about people.

MAIN CLAUSE / DEFINING RELATIVE CLAUSE

I work with clients who expect excellent service.

This relative pronoun is used for people.

The defining relative clause can also go in the middle of the main clause.

MAIN CLAUSE / DEFINING RELATIVE CLAUSE / RETURN TO MAIN CLAUSE

The clients who came to my product launch **were very impressed.**

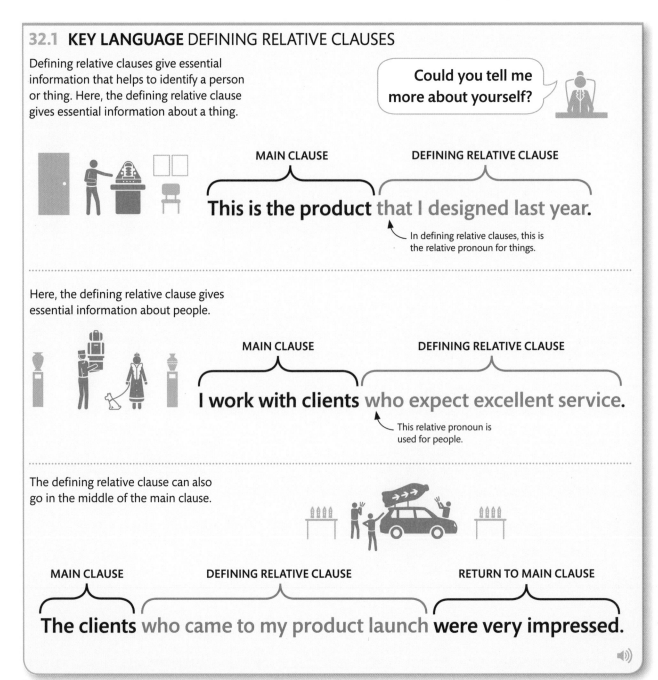

32.2 MATCH THE BEGINNINGS OF THE SENTENCES TO THE CORRECT ENDINGS

The main thing that I enjoy	is modern and open-plan.
① The office that I work in	say they enjoy working with me.
② The customers who gave us	about my job is my wonderful team.
③ One thing that I don't like	is already selling very well.
④ The people who are on my team	feedback were all very positive.
⑤ The product that we've just launched	about my job is the long hours.

32.3 CROSS OUT THE INCORRECT WORDS IN EACH SENTENCE

This is the product ~~who~~ / that / ~~what~~ I designed earlier this year. It is selling very well.

① The main thing **that** / who / where I hope to gain by working here is more experience.

② The area when / **that** / who I live in is very close to the bus routes into the business district.

③ The tasks who / when / **that** I perform best usually involve customer relations.

④ The exams why / **that** / where I passed last year mean that I am now fully qualified.

⑤ The person which / where / **who** I have learned the most from is my college professor.

⑥ The countries who / **that** / where order most of our umbrellas are in Europe.

⑦ The achievement **that** / who / where I am most proud of is winning "employee of the year."

32.4 KEY LANGUAGE NON-DEFINING RELATIVE CLAUSES

Non-defining relative clauses give extra information about situations, people, or things.

TIP
Commas separate non-defining relative clauses from main clauses.

MAIN CLAUSE   NON-DEFINING RELATIVE CLAUSE

I worked in a café, which taught me a lot about customer service.

Relative pronoun for situations in non-defining relative clauses.

Non-defining relative clauses can also go in the middle of a sentence.

MAIN CLAUSE   NON-DEFINING RELATIVE CLAUSE   RETURN TO MAIN CLAUSE

In my previous job, which was in IT, I learned how to develop apps.

Relative pronoun for things in non-defining relative clauses.

The relative pronoun for people is "who" in non-defining relative clauses.

MAIN CLAUSE   NON-DEFINING RELATIVE CLAUSE   RETURN TO MAIN CLAUSE

My clients, who have high standards, said my work was excellent.

Relative pronoun for people.

32.5 REWRITE THE SENTENCES, CORRECTING THE ERRORS

> In my current job which I have been in for three years I often give presentations.
> *In my current job, which I have been in for three years, I often give presentations.*

1 I have completed all the training, who means you wouldn't need to train me.

2 My boss, which is very talented, always encourages me not to work too late.

3 IT development, what is my favorite part of the job, is very fast-paced.

4 My co-workers who are all older than me, have taught me a lot.

5 I worked at the reception desk, that taught me how to deal with customers.

6 I take my job very seriously which means I always follow the company dress code.

7 In my last job, who was in Paris, I learned to speak French fluently.

32.6 LISTEN TO THE INTERVIEW, THEN NUMBER THE SENTENCES IN THE ORDER YOU HEAR THEM

A I work about 35 hours a week, and I love it. ☐

B I think I'm really good at understanding people's goals and aims. ☐

C I'd like to join a bigger gym so I have the opportunity to build my career. ☐

D I have 40 regular clients, who I spend 30–60 minutes with each session. ☐

E I can see you have some experience already. ☐ 1

F There are only about 100 clients, so there are only two trainers. ☐

32.7 KEY LANGUAGE MORE RELATIVE PRONOUNS

Relative clauses can use other relative pronouns, depending on the nouns they refer to.

Last summer, when I had just graduated, I did an internship at a law firm.

Use "when" to refer to a time.

The fashion industry is where I would hope to expand your client base.

Use "where" to refer to a place, industry, or sector.

My team, whose members are very motivated, always meet their targets.

Use "whose" to refer to a person, company, or department.

32.8 FILL IN THE GAPS USING THE WORDS IN THE PANEL

 My apprenticeship, _____*which*_____ I completed in 2016, was in car manufacturing.

❶ The place _____ I can concentrate the best is at home.

❷ The person _____ career inspires me the most is Muhammad Ali.

❸ Last year, _____ I was an intern, I learned how to give presentations.

❹ My parents, _____ are both doctors, inspired me to study medicine.

| where | when | ~~which~~ | who | whose |

32.9 RESPOND OUT LOUD TO THE AUDIO, FILLING IN THE GAPS USING THE PHRASES IN THE PANEL

What would you say is your biggest weakness?

People _____*who know*_____ me well say that I'm sometimes impatient.

1 What do you think of your current salary?

My current salary, _____ $20,000 a year, is not very high.

2 What do you like most about your job?

The thing _____ me excited about my job is seeing our products on sale.

3 Do you think you are a good team leader?

Yes. I always know _____ the responsibility for getting a task done on my team.

4 What benefits do you think you would bring to our company?

I can identify things _____ to change, to make your business more efficient.

5 How soon can you start, supposing we offer you the job?

My boss, _____ quite flexible, would allow me to leave after six weeks' notice.

| that need | that gets | who is | ~~who know~~ | which is | who has |

---

32 ✔ CHECKLIST

⚙ Relative clauses ☐   **Aa** Job interviews ☐   🧩 Describing your achievements in detail ☐

131

33.1 BUSINESS IDIOMS

Our company is always ahead of the game in the latest technology.

to be ahead of the game
[to be ahead of your competitors in a certain field]

This is a big contract. Make sure you do everything by the book.

to do something by the book
[to do something strictly according to the rules]

I just want to check that we are all on the same page.

to be on the same page
[to be in agreement about something]

There's been a change of pace in the company since our product launch.

a change of pace
[an increase or decrease in speed from what is normal]

I know it's always difficult to fill someone's shoes.

to fill someone's shoes
[to start doing a job or role that someone else has just left]

The design is flawed. We'll have to go back to square one.

to go back to square one
[to return to the start position]

They haven't signed the contract yet, but at least I have a foot in the door.

to get / have a foot in the door
[to gain a small initial advantage at the beginning of a longer process]

Don't complicate things. Tell me the facts in a nutshell.

in a nutshell
[simply and succinctly]

It's important to go the extra mile for these customers.

to go the extra mile
[to make more effort than is usually expected]

It's essential that we get the campaign up and running this week.

up and running
[operating properly]

I need an update on this project. Let's touch base next week.

to touch base
[to talk to someone briefly in order to catch up or get an update]

It's getting late. I think we should call it a day.

to call it a day
[to stop the current activity]

Everyone was pleased when Simon clinched the deal last week.

to clinch the deal
[to confirm or settle an agreement or contract]

We want to corner the market in street fashion by next year.

to corner the market
[to have control of a particular market]

I don't know the exact price, but I can you give you a ballpark figure.

a ballpark figure
[a rough estimate]

Food quality is extremely important in this restaurant. We can't cut corners.

to cut corners
[to do something in a cheaper or easier way, at the expense of high standards]

We're not sure which new product to launch this month. It's all up in the air.

up in the air
[uncertain and undecided]

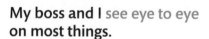

We're really behind on this project now, Tony. What's the game plan?

a game plan
[a strategy worked out beforehand]

My boss and I see eye to eye on most things.

to see eye to eye
[to agree totally]

This chair design is totally groundbreaking, Ceri.

groundbreaking
[original and a big departure from what was there before]

34 Working relationships

Phrasal verbs are commonly used to talk about relationships with co-workers and clients. It is important to use the correct word order with phrasal verbs.

🔧 **New language** Three-word phrasal verbs
Aa Vocabulary Social media
🧩 **New skill** Social networking

34.1 KEY LANGUAGE THREE-WORD PHRASAL VERBS

Three-word phrasal verbs consist of a verb and two particles. The particles usually change the meaning of the verb.

VERB AND PARTICLES

It's important to get along with clients.

34.2 FURTHER EXAMPLES THREE-WORD PHRASAL VERBS

 I look up to **my manager.**

 Caitlin looks down on **her co-workers.**

 Sadiq comes up with **great ideas.**

 I can't put up with **his loud music!**

Aa 34.3 MATCH THE DEFINITIONS TO THE PHRASAL VERBS

to accept a problem or situation

① to be as good as promised

② to be excited about something yet to happen

③ to create a particular impression

④ to escape punishment

⑤ to use all of something and not have any left

⑥ to go at the same speed as someone else

to live up to something

to keep up with someone

to face up to something

to get away with something

to run out of something

to look forward to something

to come across as something

34.4 READ THE ARTICLE AND ANSWER THE QUESTIONS

The benefits of social media were recognized quickly.
True ☐ **False** ☐ **Not given** ☑

① Not all companies think social media is useful.
True ☐ **False** ☐ **Not given** ☐

② Some companies think social media costs too much.
True ☐ **False** ☐ **Not given** ☐

③ Companies who don't use social media can compete.
True ☐ **False** ☐ **Not given** ☐

④ Customers are irritated by ads on social media.
True ☐ **False** ☐ **Not given** ☐

⑤ Social media increases awareness of brands.
True ☐ **False** ☐ **Not given** ☐

⑥ It doesn't matter if customers aren't loyal.
True ☐ **False** ☐ **Not given** ☐

Using social media
How social networking can benefit your company

Some companies have been slow to recognize the benefits of social media in business. Some even look down on social media, and doubt that it has any serious purpose or value. But ignore social media at your peril, because you can be sure your competitors are using it. And if you don't keep up with the competition, you'll never corner the market.

Using social media platforms can increase awareness of your company. Your brand becomes more familiar and more recognizable. If customers feel that they are keeping up with all your news and developments, they feel like they have a relationship with the company. As a result they become more loyal, and loyal customers make repeat purchases.

34.5 FILL IN THE GAPS USING THE WORDS IN THE PANEL

I look up ____*up*____ to Yohann. He works hard and always goes the extra mile.

① Please could you _____ up with a proposal on how to improve punctuality?

② I can't _____ up with Thom when he goes through the accounts. He's too quick.

③ Liza comes _____ as very serious, but outside of work she's a lot of fun.

④ The two interns don't get _____ with each other very well. They don't see eye to eye.

⑤ I'm really looking _____ to welcoming our new clients to London.

come	~~up~~	across	keep	forward	along

34.6 KEY LANGUAGE SEPARABLE PHRASAL VERBS WITH PRONOUNS

Some phrasal verbs are separable, which means the particle does not have to sit immediately after the verb. If the object of the sentence with a separable phrasal verb is a pronoun, it must go between the verb and the particle.

TIP
All three-word phrasal verbs are inseparable.

I'm looking up our competitors on social media. ✓

I'm looking them up on social media. ✓

I'm looking our competitors up on social media. ✓

I'm looking up them on social media. ✗

34.7 FURTHER EXAMPLES SEPARABLE PHRASAL VERBS WITH PRONOUNS

Here's a new form.
Please can you fill it in?

This is a difficult task.
Can you take it on?

They have a great website.
You must check it out.

Our clients are relying on you.
Don't let them down.

34.8 REWRITE THE SENTENCES USING OBJECT PRONOUNS

Jayne really let her co-workers down.
Jayne really let them down.

① Can you take on the presentation?

_____

② We're giving away free bags.

_____

③ Let's look up this company on social media.

_____

④ I think we should call off the meeting.

_____

⑤ Can we talk over your sales proposal?

_____

34.9 LISTEN TO THE AUDIO AND ANSWER THE QUESTIONS

Leah and Tariq are discussing how to market their products on social media.

Tariq's idea involves...

a sports event.	✓
an online survey.	☐
an advertising campaign.	☐

❶ Tariq says the company...

should spend more on advertising.	☐
needs a modern image.	☐
needs to employ more people.	☐

❷ The company could use social media to...

increase awareness of health.	☐
tell people about their products.	☐
advertise the event.	☐

❸ The event would...

encourage people to become fitter.	☐
benefit the local environment.	☐
increase awareness of the company.	☐

❹ Who will take on the work?

Tariq volunteers to do it.	☐
Leah will find a team to work on it.	☐
Leah will do the organizing.	☐

34.10 SAY THE SENTENCES OUT LOUD, CORRECTING THE ERRORS

This is a difficult task. Can you take on it?

> *This is a difficult task.*
> *Can you take it on?*

❶ I need the report today. Please don't let down me.

❷ Josef complains a lot. I can't put with it.

❸ I'm looking forward finishing my training.

❹ If you have a problem, we can talk over.

❺ Don't look down to Rachel. She's still new.

❻ Our company is giving off three cars.

34 ✓ CHECKLIST

⚙ Three-word phrasal verbs ☐   **Aa** Social media ☐   🧩 Social networking ☐

35 Career outcomes

To talk about possible future events, such as career development and promotion, use "will," "might," and "won't" to say how likely something is to happen.

⚙ **New language** Modal verbs for possibility
Aa Vocabulary Career development
🧩 **New skill** Talking about the future

35.1 KEY LANGUAGE "WILL" AND "MIGHT"

Use "will" when something is certain or very likely to happen. Use "might" for things that are possible.

Martina will add a great deal to the team.

We might need to recruit more staff.

35.2 FURTHER EXAMPLES "WILL," "MIGHT," AND "MAY"

 She will lead a team next year.

This is an alternative to "might."

You may need more training.

 Joe won't meet his sales targets.

↳ This means something is impossible or very unlikely.

 You might not get a bonus.

↳ This means something is possible but not certain.

35.3 MATCH THE PAIRS OF SENTENCES

| Staff don't understand the IT system. | → | He will be promoted to lead his team. |

1 Tanya has used up all her leave. → You may have to go to Tokyo.

2 Toby is great at managing people. → We might need to provide more training.

3 Josef doesn't get along with his boss. → She won't go on vacation this year.

4 We have some meetings in Japan. → He might not stay here much longer.

35.4 MARK THE SENTENCES THAT ARE CORRECT

Pam has more than 10 years' experience and she wills lead our sales department. ☐
Pam has more than 10 years' experience and she will lead our sales department. ☑

1. We can't hire any staff at the moment, so you don't might get an assistant until May. ☐
   We can't hire any staff at the moment, so you might not get an assistant until May. ☐

2. You're great with new staff, so we may ask you to become a mentor. ☐
   You're great with new staff, so we ask may you to become a mentor. ☐

3. It's been a bad year for the company, so you won't get a raise. ☐
   It's been a bad year for the company, so you not will get a raise. ☐

4. This report needs to be finished by Friday. You need might to work overtime. ☐
   This report needs to be finished by Friday. You might need to work overtime. ☐

5. If Lucinda's work doesn't improve, we may have to fire her. ☐
   If Lucinda's work doesn't improve, we won't have to fire her. ☐

35.5 READ THE PERFORMANCE REVIEW AND ANSWER THE QUESTIONS

Paula works in accounts.   True ☐ False ☑

1. Paula will be promoted next year.   True ☐ False ☐

2. Paula will be head of her department.   True ☐ False ☐

3. Paula will manage more than 40 people.   True ☐ False ☐

4. She won't need any extra training.   True ☐ False ☐

5. Her boss thinks she will perform well.   True ☐ False ☐

6. Paula's salary will not increase.   True ☐ False ☐

7. Paula may get a company car.   True ☐ False ☐

8. Paula will stay in the office all the time.   True ☐ False ☐

Performance Review:
Paula Stannard

Paula has worked in our customer relations department for two years. She will be promoted to assistant manager at the beginning of next year.

After her promotion, Paula will be in charge of about 45 people. We may need to give her additional training, but I am confident that she will perform well in this role. Paula will receive a 10 percent raise in her new position. We might consider providing her with a company car, as she will need to go out and visit clients.

35.6 KEY LANGUAGE "DEFINITELY" AND "PROBABLY"

Use "definitely" with "will" and "won't" to talk about things that are certain, and "probably" for things that are likely.

TIP
"Definitely" and "probably" are placed after "will" in a sentence, but before "won't."

You will definitely be promoted.

What are my chances of being promoted this year?

You will probably be promoted.

You probably won't be promoted.

You definitely won't be promoted.

35.7 REWRITE THE SENTENCES, CORRECTING THE ERRORS

You **will probable** move to the new office.
You will probably move to the new office.

1 He **don't definitely** get the job.

_____

2 You probably **don't will need** any training.

_____

3 We **will hire probably** some more staff soon.

_____

4 She **will definite** get a raise.

_____

5 I **definitely not will** move to the head office.

_____

6 I **not probably will** go on vacation this year.

_____

35.8 SAY THE SENTENCES OUT LOUD, PUTTING THE MODIFIER IN THE CORRECT PLACE

You won't get a new laptop. [definitely]

You definitely won't get a new laptop.

1 We will get a thank-you gift. [probably]

2 I won't change jobs this year. [definitely]

3 You will get a bonus. [definitely]

4 We won't invite him to the meeting. [probably]

35.9 LISTEN TO THE AUDIO AND MATCH THE IMAGES TO THE CORRECT PHRASES

| definitely won't happen | will definitely happen | may happen | might not happen | probably won't happen |

---

35 ✓ CHECKLIST

⚙ Modal verbs for possibility ☐   **Aa** Career development ☐   🧩 Talking about the future ☐

🔄 REVIEW THE ENGLISH YOU HAVE LEARNED IN UNITS 30–35

NEW LANGUAGE	SAMPLE SENTENCE	☑	UNIT
"A" AND "THE"	I applied for a job as a nurse. The application form was really long.	☐	30.1
DEFINITE AND ZERO ARTICLES FOR PLURALS	Accountants work very hard. The accountants in my office work long hours.	☐	30.4, 30.5
DEPENDENT PREPOSITIONS	I worked with the head chef in a restaurant.	☐	31.1, 31.6
RELATIVE CLAUSES	This is the product that I designed last year. I worked in a café, which was a lot of fun.	☐	32.1, 32.5
THREE-WORD PHRASAL VERBS	It's important to get along with clients.	☐	34.1
PHRASAL VERBS WITH PRONOUNS	Here's a form. Please can you fill it in?	☐	34.6, 34.7
TALKING ABOUT POSSIBILITIES	We might have to recruit more staff. You will definitely be promoted.	☐	35.1, 35.6

36.1 OFFICE AND PRESENTATION EQUIPMENT

computer

screen

keyboard

mouse

laptop

tablet

touch screen

cursor

power button

charger

power cable

low battery

USB drive / flash drive

hard drive

router

laminator

scanner

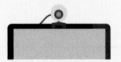

webcam

video camera

voice recorder

printer

slides

handout

projector

projector screen

lectern

clicker

pointer

cue cards

microphone

speakers

chairs

flipchart

whiteboard

erasable markers

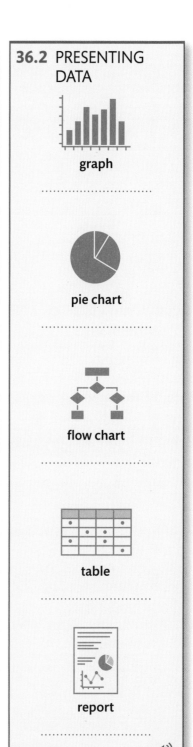

36.2 PRESENTING DATA

graph

pie chart

flow chart

table

report

Structuring a presentation

When you are presenting to an audience, it is important to structure your talk in a way that is clear and easy to understand. Certain set phrases can help you do this.

⚙ **New language** Signposting language
Aa Vocabulary Presentation equipment
🧩 **New skill** Structuring a presentation

37.1 KEY LANGUAGE SIGNPOSTING LANGUAGE

You can signal (or "signpost") what you are going to talk about with particular phrases. Using these lets your audience know what to expect.

Giving the audience the format of the talk.

We'll look at the data, then I'll take questions.

Introducing the topic of the talk.

My talk today is about reducing our energy bills.

Ending one section.

So, we've looked at the main difficulty facing us.

Starting a new section.

Let's now turn to the potential solutions.

Summarizing the content of the talk.

To sum up, we have to cut costs across the board.

Asking the audience for questions.

Do feel free to ask any questions.

37.2 LISTEN TO THE AUDIO AND ANSWER THE QUESTIONS

 The owner of a café is presenting proposals for the future to the investors.

The speaker invites questions during the talk.	True ☐	False ☑	Not given ☐
❶ The café is not very successful.	True ☐	False ☐	Not given ☐
❷ One option is adding 20 more tables.	True ☐	False ☐	Not given ☐
❸ Any expansion would require more restrooms.	True ☐	False ☐	Not given ☐
❹ The choice is to expand or close the café.	True ☐	False ☐	Not given ☐
❺ The speaker wants to expand the café.	True ☐	False ☐	Not given ☐

 37.3 REWRITE THE SENTENCES, PUTTING THE WORDS IN THE CORRECT ORDER

talk. | end | my | That | me | brings | the | to | of

That brings me to the end of my talk.

❶ up, | bright | To | a | future. | sum | have | we | very

_____

❷ ask | questions. | feel | me | Do | to | any | free

_____

❸ the | figures. | turn | predicted | Let's | sales | to

_____

❹ we've | alternatives. | looked | all | So, | at | main | the

_____

145

Aa 37.4 MATCH THE DEFINITIONS TO THE EQUIPMENT

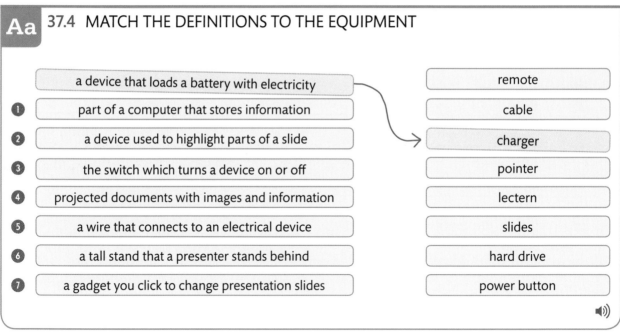

a device that loads a battery with electricity → charger

1. part of a computer that stores information
2. a device used to highlight parts of a slide
3. the switch which turns a device on or off
4. projected documents with images and information
5. a wire that connects to an electrical device
6. a tall stand that a presenter stands behind
7. a gadget you click to change presentation slides

remote
cable
charger
pointer
lectern
slides
hard drive
power button

37.5 SAY THE SENTENCES OUT LOUD, FILLING IN THE GAPS WITH THE WORDS IN THE PANEL

You can ask for copies of the _____slides_____ after the talk.

1. Be careful of the _____ in front of the stage.

2. I will return to the _____ to answer questions.

3. If you follow my _____, you can see the graph.

4. I'll use my _____ to forward to the final slide.

5. This projector's noisy. I'll turn the _____ off.

cable   ~~slides~~   lectern   pointer   remote   power button

37.6 READ THE ARTICLE AND ANSWER THE QUESTIONS

> We often see similar pictures in presentations.
> **True** ☑ **False** ☐ **Not given** ☐

1 Images always make presentations exciting.
True ☐ **False** ☐ **Not given** ☐

2 The writer often gives presentations himself.
True ☐ **False** ☐ **Not given** ☐

3 Slides can add extra meaning to the presentation.
True ☐ **False** ☐ **Not given** ☐

4 It can be better to use your own images.
True ☐ **False** ☐ **Not given** ☐

5 It is better to have a lot of text on slides.
True ☐ **False** ☐ **Not given** ☐

6 You must have slides to give a good presentation.
True ☐ **False** ☐ **Not given** ☐

PRESENTATIONS AND TALKS

Visual Aids: tips and tricks

Make the most of the images you use in your presentations

The internet contains millions of images and yet, when we sit through presentations, we often see the same old pictures of cogs and handshakes. These images add little value to any presentation. Here are some simple tips for using visual aids in presentations. First, use clear slides with simple images that add to the meaning of the presentation. Also, don't forget that you can use your own photographs, rather than the impersonal images taken from the internet. Next, ensure that slides are not covered in lots of tiny text that is either difficult to read, or that you intend to read out anyway. Finally, consider if you need slides at all. If they don't add anything, you may be better off without them.

37.7 LISTEN TO THE AUDIO, THEN NUMBER THE SENTENCES IN THE ORDER YOU HEAR THEM

A My talk today is about the advertising budget for the next year. ☐

B Let's now turn to the advertising plans for next year. ☐

C Do feel free to ask any questions or for more information. ☐

D Good morning. Thank you for coming to my presentation this morning. [1]

E So, we've looked at last year's advertising successes and failures. ☐

F To sum up, we will have even more publicity for less money. ☐

G If you follow my pointer, you'll see last year's figures on the left. ☐

H I'll quickly go through the figures and then I'll take any questions. ☐

37 ✓ CHECKLIST

⚙ Signposting language ☐   **Aa** Presentation equipment ☐   🧩 Structuring a presentation ☐

38 Developing an argument

When you are giving a presentation, there are several key phrases you can use to develop your argument, and make your audience aware of what is coming.

⚙ **New language** Useful presentation language
Aa Vocabulary Presentations
🧩 **New skill** Developing an argument

38.1 KEY LANGUAGE GENERALIZING, MAKING EXCEPTIONS, AND FOCUSING

If you have specific figures, it may be useful to give them.
However, you may need to use more general terms if you do not have the figures or you want to avoid repetition.

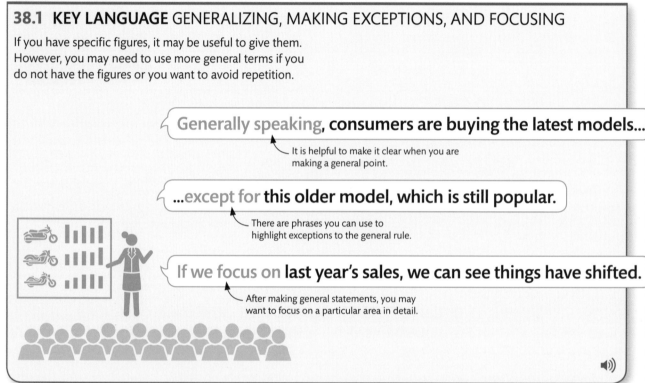

Generally speaking, consumers are buying the latest models...
It is helpful to make it clear when you are making a general point.

...except for this older model, which is still popular.
There are phrases you can use to highlight exceptions to the general rule.

If we focus on last year's sales, we can see things have shifted.
After making general statements, you may want to focus on a particular area in detail.

38.2 WRITE THE PHRASES FROM THE PANEL IN THE CORRECT CATEGORIES

GENERALIZING	EXCEPTIONS	FOCUSING
on the whole	_____	_____
_____	_____	_____
_____	_____	_____
_____	_____	_____

except for   with the exception of

generally   if we focus on

aside from   ~~on the whole~~

if we home in on   excepting

concentrating on   focusing on

in general   by and large

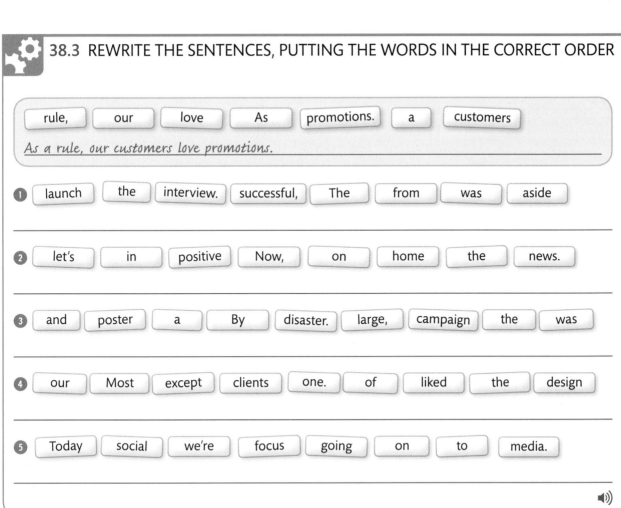

38.3 REWRITE THE SENTENCES, PUTTING THE WORDS IN THE CORRECT ORDER

| rule, | our | love | As | promotions. | a | customers |

As a rule, our customers love promotions.

1. launch / the / interview. / successful, / The / from / was / aside

_____

2. let's / in / positive / Now, / on / home / the / news.

_____

3. and / poster / a / By / disaster. / large, / campaign / the / was

_____

4. our / Most / except / clients / one. / of / liked / the / design

_____

5. Today / social / we're / focus / going / on / to / media.

_____

38.4 LISTEN TO THE AUDIO AND ANSWER THE QUESTIONS

A brand manager is talking to an audience about a new range of products.

ValenTova's is going to take over Tina's.
True ☐ **False** ☑ **Not given** ☐

1. Both brands have a good reputation.
True ☐ **False** ☐ **Not given** ☐

2. The new partnership will have a website.
True ☐ **False** ☐ **Not given** ☐

3. You can only buy Tina's in London.
True ☐ **False** ☐ **Not given** ☐

4. They will sell mail order chocolate.
True ☐ **False** ☐ **Not given** ☐

5. The ice cream will be called Valentina's.
True ☐ **False** ☐ **Not given** ☐

38.5 KEY LANGUAGE GIVING EXAMPLES

When you have focused your argument, you may want to give examples to explain your point.

"For instance" can go at the beginning, middle, or (less commonly) end of a sentence.

For instance, our new distribution method has been a huge success.

You can also say "As an illustration..." at the start of a sentence.

As an example, our products have been very popular in Asia.

We've made progress in new sectors such as the travel market.

"Such as" comes in the middle of a sentence before the noun it is illustrating.

38.6 KEY LANGUAGE COUNTERING THE GENERAL OPINION

To counter something that has been stated as, or is understood as, the general opinion there are a number of set phrases you can use.

These phrases tend to go at the beginning of sentences.

In fact...

Actually...

As a matter of fact...

In actual fact...

In reality...

However...

38.7 READ THE ARTICLE AND ANSWER THE QUESTIONS

	True	False
The article is about creating slides.	☐	☑
❶ Start with a joke.	True ☐	False ☐
❷ Research each audience.	True ☐	False ☐
❸ You should not stay still.	True ☐	False ☐
❹ You should look serious.	True ☐	False ☐

15 LIFE HACKS

PRESENTING

We put a lot of effort into writing presentations, so it's important to keep the audience's attention. Start with a good, relevant story and include facts and images that are aimed directly at your audience. This shows you have researched them and their needs. Use the space that you have and move around the stage. Lastly, make sure that you look up regularly and smile.

38.8 RESPOND OUT LOUD TO THE AUDIO, FILLING IN THE GAPS USING THE WORDS IN THE PANEL

How do our customers spend their free time?

> Our research shows that, _____as a rule_____ , they are very active.

1 So, were all the media campaigns failures?

> No. _____ the posters, we can see they were very successful.

2 Did all the stores improve sales last year?

> Yes, _____ our Madrid store.

3 So, it was yet another poor year for the company.

> _____ it was very successful.

4 Where do you think we should open the next store?

> Cities _____ Seoul and Busan could have successful stores.

5 Have sales increased after the launch of our new TV advert?

> They haven't yet. _____ , it's too soon to see what the impact will be.

If we focus on   As a matter of fact   However   ~~as a rule~~   such as   with the exception of

---

38 ✓ CHECKLIST

⚙ Useful presentation language ☐   **Aa** Presentations ☐   🧩 Developing an argument ☐

When describing a product to a potential client, it is useful to compare the product with competitors using comparative and superlative adjectives.

⚙ **New language** Comparatives and superlatives
Aa Vocabulary Product marketing
🧩 **New skill** Comparing products

39.1 KEY LANGUAGE COMPARATIVE AND SUPERLATIVE ADJECTIVES

Regular comparative adjectives are formed by adding "-er" to the adjective. Regular superlatives are formed by adding "the" before and "-est" after the adjective.

Comparative

Our competitors might offer cheaper broadband, but ours is the fastest.

Superlative

For some two-syllable adjectives, and all adjectives with more than two syllables, add "more" before the adjective to make the comparative, and "the most" to make the superlative.

This sports car is more stylish than anything else on the market, and the most beautiful car on sale today.

🔊

39.2 FURTHER EXAMPLES COMPARATIVE AND SUPERLATIVE ADJECTIVES

Our new widescreen TV is bigger than any other flatscreen TV.

We offer better customer service than any of our competitors.

These are the easiest tents to put up and take down.

Nevastick 3000 is, quite simply, the best frying pan I've ever used.

🔊

39.3 REWRITE THE SENTENCES, CORRECTING THE ERRORS

> Our phones are much more reliabler than our competitors' phones.
> *Our phones are much more reliable than our competitors' phones.*

❶ Our new smartwatch is easyer to operate than the old one.

_____

❷ Our new designer jeans are stylish than last year's products.

_____

❸ Our tablet is cheapest on the market.

_____

❹ This is the more beautiful dress in our range.

_____

❺ This is the goodest laptop I have ever owned.

_____

🔊

39.4 LISTEN TO THE AUDIO AND MATCH THE PRODUCTS TO THE PHRASES THAT DESCRIBE THEM

| the most reliable | the thinnest | more affordable | lighter | more comfortable |

39.5 KEY LANGUAGE "AS... AS" COMPARISONS

English uses "as... as" with an adjective to compare things that are similar.

Our laptops are as fast as our competitors' laptops, but are much cheaper.

◀))

39.6 FURTHER EXAMPLES "AS... AS" COMPARISONS

Use "just as... as" to emphasize the similarity between two things.

Our new watch is just as light as any other design on the market.

Use "not as... as" to contrast things that are different.

This drill is not as noisy as many existing brands.

This sports drink is as healthy as the leading brand, but much cheaper.

Our washing machine is as quick as more expensive models.

◀))

39.7 MARK THE SENTENCES THAT ARE CORRECT

These energy-efficient light bulbs are just as effective as the old ones. ☑

These energy-efficient light bulbs are as just effective as the old ones. ☐

1 Our new phone is cheap as existing models, but has a much wider range of features. ☐

Our new phone is as cheap as existing models, but has a much wider range of features. ☐

2 Our latest DVD is as more exciting as anything I've ever seen. ☐

Our latest DVD is as exciting as anything I've ever seen. ☐

3 Our chairs are excellent value, and just as comfortable as more expensive models. ☐

Our chairs are excellent value, and as just as comfortable as more expensive models. ☐

◀))

GARDENER'S WEEKLY

ORGANIC VEG BOX

Perfect organic goodness, delivered to your door

In our veg box, you'll find the freshest lettuce, picked the day before delivery, and delicious, ripe, seasonal fruit. You and your family will love it!

Our vegetables are just as cheap as supermarket produce. And we deliver them free to your door every week!

Vegetables in the box are grown in the UK.
True ☐ False ☐ Not given ☑

❶ The ad claims that the fruit tastes delicious.
True ☐ False ☐ Not given ☐

❷ The veg box contains apples.
True ☐ False ☐ Not given ☐

❸ Vegetables in the supermarket are cheaper.
True ☐ False ☐ Not given ☐

❹ There is no extra charge for home delivery.
True ☐ False ☐ Not given ☐

❺ The box is available in different sizes.
True ☐ False ☐ Not given ☐

39.9 CROSS OUT THE INCORRECT WORDS IN EACH SENTENCE, THEN SAY THE SENTENCES OUT LOUD

This car is ~~reliabler~~ / **more reliable** than other models, and good value for money.

❶ Our new laptop is much **lighter** / **more light** than its competitors.

❷ This fitness tracker is **just effective as** / **just as effective as** more expensive models.

❸ Organic fruit is not **as cheap** / **as cheap as** supermarket fruit, but it tastes better.

❹ A consumer survey voted our pizzas the **tastiest** / **most tastyest** on the market.

39 ✓ CHECKLIST

⚙ Comparatives and superlatives ☐   Aa Product marketing ☐   🧩 Comparing products ☐

Talking about facts and figures

When you are making a presentation or writing a report, it is important to describe changes and trends with precise language that sounds natural.

🔧 **New language** Collocations
Aa Vocabulary Business trends
🧩 **New skill** Describing facts and figures

40.1 KEY LANGUAGE DESCRIBING TRENDS WITH COLLOCATIONS

You can use a verb modified with an adverb to describe the speed or size of a change. Some of these pairings are collocations that sound "right" to fluent speakers.

TIP
Collocations are often formed of two words, but can contain more. Using them will make you a more fluent English speaker.

VERB   ADVERB

Sales have declined considerably.

House prices are fluctuating wildly.

Public interest has fallen steadily.

The markets have rallied slightly.

Some collocations to describe trends are adjectives followed by a noun.

ADJECTIVE   NOUN

There was a steady increase last quarter.

We expect a considerable drop in the new year.

After the news, there was a dramatic spike in sales.

There was a sharp rise in profits over the winter.

🔊

40.2 LISTEN TO THE AUDIO, THEN NUMBER THE TRENDS IN THE ORDER THEY ARE DESCRIBED

 A ☐

 B ☐ 1

 C ☐

 D ☐

 E ☐

 F ☐

 G ☐

 H ☐

40.3 MATCH THE PAIRS OF SENTENCES THAT MEAN THE SAME THING

Profits are going to increase a lot.

We've had a sharp rise in customer numbers.

Sales of our bags have rallied slightly.

We expect a sharp rise in profits.

① Our share value has increased gradually.

② There was much less interested in our bags.

③ There have been many more customers.

④ Sales increased suddenly in May.

⑤ People are a bit more interested in our bags.

⑥ There's been a steady decline in share value.

⑦ The dollar's value is going up and down.

⑧ The value of the dollar increased a lot.

The value of the dollar saw a dramatic spike.

Interest in our bags declined considerably.

The value of the dollar is fluctuating wildly.

There was a dramatic spike in sales in May.

The value of our shares has fallen steadily.

There was a steady increase in our share value.

🔊

40.4 VOCABULARY DESCRIBING FIGURES USING PREPOSITIONS

Between 25 and 30 percent of our stock is seasonal.

....

Sales have fallen by 40 percent in the last quarter.

....

There was an increase of 5 percent, with profits peaking at $20 per unit.

....

We are increasing our fleet from 20 cars to 35.

....

40.5 CROSS OUT THE INCORRECT WORD IN EACH SENTENCE

We expect the price to stay ~~from~~ / at $500.

1. Returns have increased **by** / at 10 percent.

2. Prices fell between 30 **and** / of 45 percent.

3. We're shrinking our staff **from** / at 800 to 650.

4. Year-end profit stands in / **at** 8 percent.

5. Salaries will increase **by** / of 2 percent.

6. We have **between** / after 1,100 and 1,200 staff.

7. There was a decrease **of** / on 5 percent.

8. Profits have fallen for / **by** 15 percent.

9. We are lowering the price **to** / at 30 euros.

10. The price peaked in / **at** £19.99.

40.6 READ THE REPORT AND ANSWER THE QUESTIONS

The share price has fallen a lot.
True ✓ **False** ☐ **Not given** ☐

1. The share price was £22 when the markets closed.
True ☐ **False** ☐ **Not given** ☐

2. There was a small increase in share prices after 11am.
True ☐ **False** ☐ **Not given** ☐

3. RedJet's tickets are likely to become more expensive.
True ☐ **False** ☐ **Not given** ☐

4. RedJet's tickets are 10 percent cheaper than average.
True ☐ **False** ☐ **Not given** ☐

FLIGHT FRIGHT

Share prices in the aviation company RedJet plummeted overnight after news emerged that its home airport—Stanmore—will be tightening security further, making it difficult for the company to offer as many flights. The company's share price dropped by 27 percent to £22 when the markets opened. Confidence had returned slightly by 11am, when the price climbed slightly to £23.50.

Stanmore airport has also said that it will increase the landing fee it charges RedJet from £1,100 to £1,300 per plane. This means the low-budget airline will almost certainly have to increase ticket prices by between 5 and 10 percent.

40.7 SAY THE SENTENCES OUT LOUD, FILLING IN THE GAPS USING THE WORDS IN THE PANEL

Last year, our sales _declined steadily_ .

② It's been _____ since the announcement.

① There was a _____ at the start of the year.

③ We're expecting them to _____ next quarter.

| fluctuating wildly | rally considerably | ~~declined steadily~~ | sharp increase |

40 ✓ CHECKLIST

⚙ Collocations ☐   **Aa** Business trends ☐   🧩 Describing facts and figures ☐

🔄 REVIEW THE ENGLISH YOU HAVE LEARNED IN UNITS 36–40

NEW LANGUAGE	SAMPLE SENTENCE	✓	UNIT
STRUCTURING A PRESENTATION	So, we've looked at the main difficulty facing us. Let's now turn to some solutions.	☐	37.1
GENERALIZING, MAKING EXCEPTIONS, AND FOCUSING	Generally speaking, customers are buying the latest models, except for this old model.	☐	38.1
GIVING EXAMPLES AND COUNTERING	For instance, our new distribution model has been a huge success.	☐	38.5, 38.6
PITCHING A PRODUCT WITH COMPARATIVES AND SUPERLATIVES	Our competitors might offer cheaper broadband, but ours is the fastest.	☐	39.1, 39.5
DESCRIBING TRENDS	Sales have declined considerably. There was a steady increase.	☐	40.1
DESCRIBING FIGURES USING PREPOSITIONS	Between 25 and 30 percent of our stock is seasonal.	☐	40.4

English uses modal verbs to make suggestions, and indirect questions or the passive voice to politely request information or point out a mistake.

⚙ **New language** Indirect questions
Aa Vocabulary Business negotiations
🧩 **New skill** Negotiating politely

41.1 KEY LANGUAGE NEGOTIATION AND SUGGESTIONS

One way of making language for negotiation more polite and indirect is to use modal verbs or the past continuous.

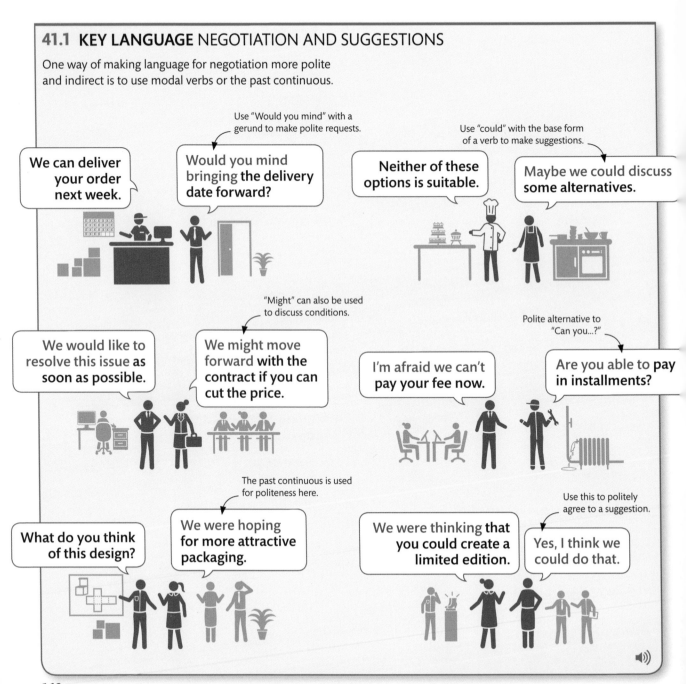

We can deliver your order next week.

Use "Would you mind" with a gerund to make polite requests.

Would you mind bringing **the delivery date forward?**

Neither of these options is suitable.

Use "could" with the base form of a verb to make suggestions.

Maybe we could discuss **some alternatives.**

We would like to resolve this issue **as soon as possible.**

"Might" can also be used to discuss conditions.

We might move forward **with the contract if you can cut the price.**

I'm afraid we can't pay your fee now.

Polite alternative to "Can you...?"

Are you able to **pay in installments?**

What do you think of this design?

The past continuous is used for politeness here.

We were hoping **for more attractive packaging.**

We were thinking **that you could create a limited edition.**

Use this to politely agree to a suggestion.

Yes, I think we could do that.

41.2 MARK THE MOST POLITE REPLY TO EACH STATEMENT

I'm afraid we're not going to meet your deadline.

Are you able to finish by the end of the month? ☑

That's terrible news. ☐

1 We were thinking that you could design a gift box.

Yes, I think we could do that. ☐

That sounds complicated. ☐

2 I would like to resolve the issue right away.

We can't agree anything without a delivery date. ☐

We might move forward if we can agree on a delivery date. ☐

3 Our client doesn't like these colors.

We'll have to start again. ☐

Maybe we could consider different colors. ☐

4 My payment terms are 30 days.

I can't pay you until next month. ☐

Would you mind waiting until next month for payment? ☐

5 What do you think of our new product?

We were hoping it would be more innovative. ☐

It's too old-fashioned. ☐

🔊

41.3 LISTEN TO THE AUDIO AND ANSWER THE QUESTIONS

Kevin is negotiating with Jamila, whose catering company might provide refreshments for an event.

How many people will be at the party?
100 people ☐
150 people ☑
200 people ☐

1 What is the maximum number of people the company can cater for?
500 ☐
1,000 ☐
1,500 ☐

2 What does Kevin say the problem with the price is?
It doesn't include drinks ☐
It is for 35 people ☐
It is too high ☐

3 What else does Kevin ask the company to supply for the party?
A cake ☐
A design ☐
A table layout ☐

4 When will Kevin talk to Jamila again?
Tomorrow ☐
Next week ☐
Next month ☐

41.4 KEY LANGUAGE INDIRECT QUESTIONS

Indirect questions start with a polite opening phrase. Unlike with direct questions, the verb sits after the subject in indirect questions.

Indirect questions start with a polite opening phrase.

Could you tell me **when my order** will **be ready?**

[When will my order be ready?]

Direct questions and indirect questions follow a different word order.

41.5 FURTHER EXAMPLES INDIRECT QUESTIONS

If the opening phrase is "Could you tell me," the indirect question ends with a question mark.

Could you tell me **how much your product** costs?

Indirect questions leave out the auxiliary verb "do."

If the opening phrase is "I was wondering," the indirect question ends with a period (full stop).

I was wondering **what time your store** closes.

Could you tell me **when we** can **expect payment?**

I was wondering **if you** are **free for a meeting.**

41.6 HOW TO FORM INDIRECT QUESTIONS

OPENING PHRASE	QUESTION WORD	SUBJECT	VERB
Could you tell me	when	the store	closes?

You can also use "I was wondering."

In indirect questions, the verb follows the subject.

REWRITE THE SENTENCES, PUTTING THE WORDS IN THE CORRECT ORDER

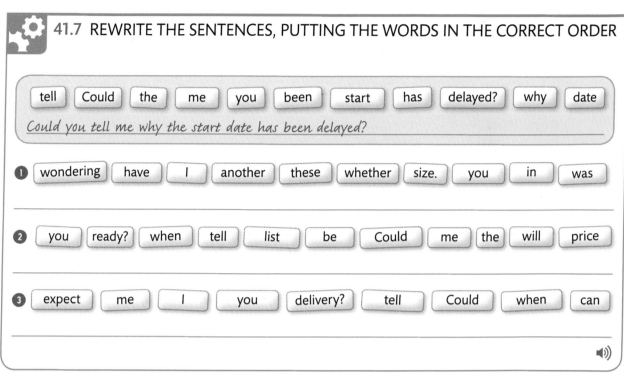

tell | Could | the | me | you | been | start | has | delayed? | why | date

Could you tell me why the start date has been delayed?

1 wondering | have | I | another | these | whether | size. | you | in | was

_____

2 you | ready? | when | tell | list | be | Could | me | the | will | price

_____

3 expect | me | I | you | delivery? | tell | Could | when | can

_____

41.8 SAY THE SENTENCES OUT LOUD, CORRECTING THE ERRORS

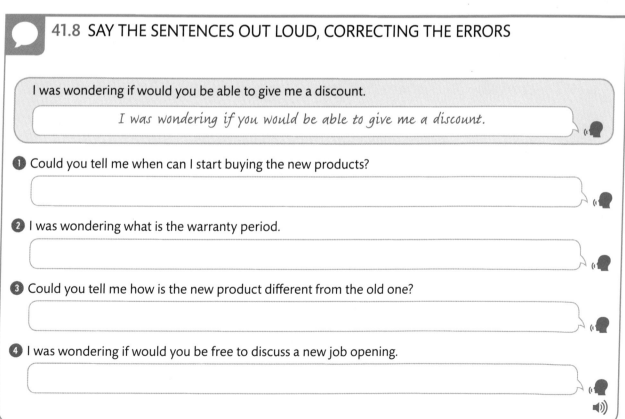

I was wondering if would you be able to give me a discount.

I was wondering if you would be able to give me a discount.

1 Could you tell me when can I start buying the new products?

2 I was wondering what is the warranty period.

3 Could you tell me how is the new product different from the old one?

4 I was wondering if would you be free to discuss a new job opening.

163

41.9 KEY LANGUAGE THE PASSIVE VOICE

In formal or written negotiations or complaints, you can use
the passive voice to be polite and avoid sounding too critical.

It seems that a mistake has been made.

[You made a mistake.]

Complaints using the passive voice often
start with a polite opening phrase.

I'm afraid the invoice was not paid on time.

[You didn't pay the invoice on time.]

It looks as if your staff are
not very well trained.

[You don't train your staff very well.]

41.10 REWRITE THE SENTENCES USING THE PASSIVE VOICE

I'm afraid you delivered our order several days late.
I'm afraid our order was delivered several days late.

1 Could you tell me whether you have changed the delivery date?

_____

2 I was wondering whether you have paid my invoice.

_____

3 It seems that you sent the wrong product.

_____

4 It looks as if that you did not fully understand my complaint.

_____

5 It seems that you did not calculate the price correctly.

_____

Aa 41.11 MATCH THE BEGINNINGS OF THE SENTENCES TO THE CORRECT ENDINGS

We would like to resolve	the sales start?
1 I'm afraid I can't access	the discount has not been applied.
2 It looks as if	→ this issue as soon as possible.
3 I was wondering why the	the computer system right now.
4 Could you tell me when	has been contacted.
5 It seems that the wrong customer	deadline has been missed.

🔊

41.12 READ THE EMAIL AND ANSWER THE QUESTIONS

Bettina's order arrived on May 5.
True ☐ False ☐ Not given ☑

1 The shipments from Ms. Liang are often late.
True ☐ False ☐ Not given ☐

2 Ms. Liang said the order was sent before April 26.
True ☐ False ☐ Not given ☐

3 Bettina has the shipping information.
True ☐ False ☐ Not given ☐

4 Ms. Liang won't be charged for the late delivery.
True ☐ False ☐ Not given ☐

5 Bettina will cancel her next order.
True ☐ False ☐ Not given ☐

✉   ⌄ ✕

To: Jennifer Liang

Subject: Shipment of jeans overdue

Dear Ms. Liang,

I'm afraid we have still not received the shipment of jeans that was due to arrive on May 5. I contacted you on April 26, when you confirmed that the order had been sent and would arrive on time. Could you please send me the shipping information and tell me when the order will arrive?

I'm afraid we will have to make a deduction from your final invoice to compensate us for the late delivery.

I look forward to hearing from you,
Bettina Koehl

↩ ↩↩   📎 🗑

41 ✓ CHECKLIST

⚙ Indirect questions ☐   **Aa** Business negotiations ☐   🧩 Negotiating politely ☐

42 Emphasizing your opinion

There are many English phrases for politely emphasizing your point of view. These are useful when you are dealing with disagreement in the workplace.

⚙ **New language** Discourse markers for emphasis
Aa Vocabulary Workplace disagreement
🧩 **New skill** Emphasizing your opinion

42.1 KEY LANGUAGE DISCOURSE MARKERS FOR EMPHASIS

There are a variety of words and phrases that you can use to make your position more emphatic without being rude.

Is there any reason why you can't sign the contract today?

What we need is **an assurance from you about the future.**

42.2 FURTHER EXAMPLES DISCOURSE MARKERS FOR EMPHASIS

Could we see some more options for the design tomorrow?

Actually, we are very short-staffed at the moment. Would next week be OK?

I'm afraid your asking price is too high.

If you ask me, **this is a good deal for you.**

42.3 CROSS OUT THE INCORRECT WORDS IN EACH SENTENCE

What I'm ~~needing~~ / saying / ~~telling~~ is that we need to increase sales by at least five percent.

 1 If you ask I / me / us, we might be better to wait until the summer.

2 Which / Who / What we need is proof that your business is profitable.

3 Actually / Actual / Actionally, we'd like to reach an agreement by the end of the day.

4 The main / most / minor thing is that we agree on a price that everyone is happy with.

42.4 LISTEN TO THE NEGOTIATION, THEN NUMBER THE SENTENCES IN THE ORDER YOU HEAR THEM

A If you ask me, these colors are quite bright already. ☐

B We need assurance that you can supply 1,000 umbrellas a month. ☐

C Actually, we're worried about the colors. ☐ 1

D The main thing is that our company logo should really stand out. ☐

E What I'm saying is I can send you samples in brighter colors next week. ☐

42.5 RESPOND OUT LOUD TO THE AUDIO, FILLING IN THE GAPS USING THE WORDS IN THE PANEL

Is there any chance you could reduce your asking price?

I'm afraid not. If _____*you ask me*_____ , you won't find a lower price.

1 Are you ready to sign the contract?

Not quite. _____ some references from your customers.

2 I'm afraid I can't start on this job until December.

That's OK. The _____ we find the right person to do the work.

3 Is it possible for you to offer free delivery?

_____ , our quote already includes free delivery.

| What we need are | ~~you ask me~~ | Actually | main thing is that |

42 ✓ CHECKLIST

⚙ Discourse markers for emphasis ☐   **Aa** Workplace disagreement ☐   🏃 Emphasizing your opinion ☐

43 Discussing conditions

English often uses the first and second conditionals for negotiating with clients and co-workers, and the zero conditional to talk about general truths.

🔧 **New language** Conditionals
Aa Vocabulary Negotiating and bargaining
🧩 **New skill** Discussing possibilities

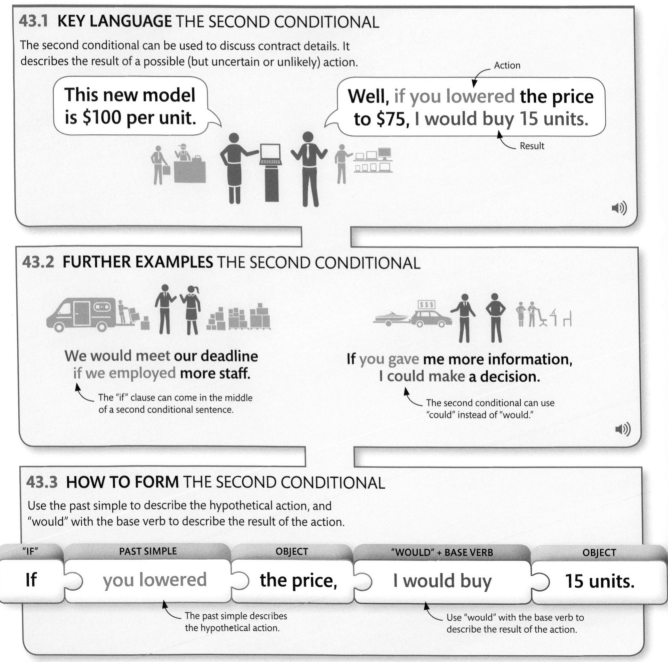

43.1 KEY LANGUAGE THE SECOND CONDITIONAL

The second conditional can be used to discuss contract details. It describes the result of a possible (but uncertain or unlikely) action.

Action

This new model is $100 per unit.

Well, **if you lowered** the price to $75, **I would buy 15 units.**

Result

43.2 FURTHER EXAMPLES THE SECOND CONDITIONAL

We **would meet** our deadline **if we employed** more staff.

The "if" clause can come in the middle of a second conditional sentence.

If you gave me more information, **I could make** a decision.

The second conditional can use "could" instead of "would."

43.3 HOW TO FORM THE SECOND CONDITIONAL

Use the past simple to describe the hypothetical action, and "would" with the base verb to describe the result of the action.

"IF"	PAST SIMPLE	OBJECT	"WOULD" + BASE VERB	OBJECT
If	you lowered	the price,	I would buy	15 units.

The past simple describes the hypothetical action.

Use "would" with the base verb to describe the result of the action.

43.4 REWRITE THE SECOND CONDITIONAL SENTENCES, CORRECTING THE ERRORS

If you give me a discount, I would book.
If you gave me a discount, I would book.

1 I would placed an order if they delivered sooner.

_____

2 If your product is cheaper, we would buy it.

_____

3 If you moved the deadline, we could to meet it.

_____

4 I work with them if they answered my questions.

_____

5 If they would check their work, I would use them.

_____

🔊

43.5 LISTEN TO THE AUDIO AND ANSWER THE QUESTIONS

Diane is negotiating a better price for her office supplies with Josef, an office stationery salesman.

Diane has talked to another company.
True ☑ **False** ☐ **Not given** ☐

1 Diane is impressed with Office Hub's offers.
True ☐ **False** ☐ **Not given** ☐

2 Diane has always bought stationery from Josef.
True ☐ **False** ☐ **Not given** ☐

3 Josef can't offer free next-day delivery.
True ☐ **False** ☐ **Not given** ☐

4 Josef offers free delivery after four days.
True ☐ **False** ☐ **Not given** ☐

5 The two-for-one deal is a new offer.
True ☐ **False** ☐ **Not given** ☐

43.6 COMPLETE THESE SECOND CONDITIONAL SENTENCES, SAYING THEM OUT LOUD

If you _offered_ (offer) a discount,
I _would order_ (order) now.

1 We _____ (sign) the contract
if it _____ (be) clearer.

2 I _____ (accept) the job offer
if the pay _____ (be) better.

3 If they _____ (improve) the quality,
we _____ (place) an order.

4 If I _____ (have) more time today,
I _____ (check) the contract.

🔊

169

43.7 KEY LANGUAGE ZERO AND FIRST CONDITIONALS

THE ZERO CONDITIONAL

Use the zero conditional to talk about things that are generally true. The present simple describes the action and the result.

PRESENT SIMPLE

PRESENT SIMPLE

If customers buy our products in bulk, we reduce our prices.

⌐ Action

⌐ Result

THE FIRST CONDITIONAL

The first conditional uses the present simple and the future with "will" to talk about the likely results of things that might happen.

PRESENT SIMPLE

FUTURE WITH "WILL"

If you are not satisfied, we will give you a refund.

⌐ Action

⌐ Result

43.8 FURTHER EXAMPLES ZERO AND FIRST CONDITIONALS

Zero conditional sentences can use "when" instead of "if."

When we work too late, we're tired the next day.

Conditional sentences can start with the result clause.

You'll get a bonus if your presentation goes well.

Products don't sell well if they're poor quality.

If you don't plan ahead, you won't have enough stock.

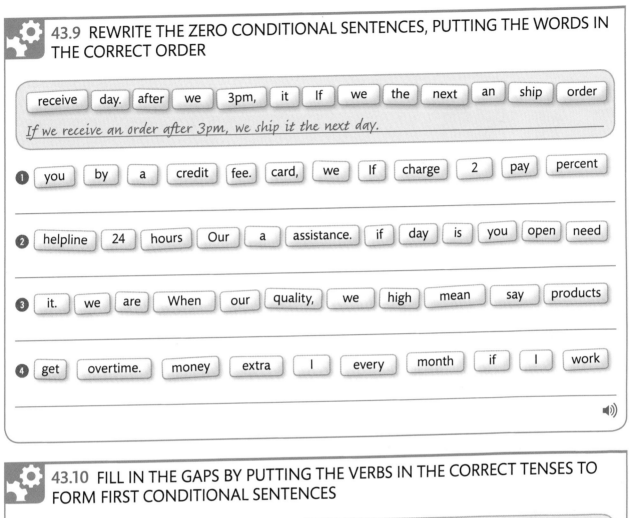

43.9 REWRITE THE ZERO CONDITIONAL SENTENCES, PUTTING THE WORDS IN THE CORRECT ORDER

receive | day. | after | we | 3pm, | it | If | we | the | next | an | ship | order

If we receive an order after 3pm, we ship it the next day.

1. you | by | a | credit | fee. | card, | we | If | charge | 2 | pay | percent

_____

2. helpline | 24 | hours | Our | a | assistance. | if | day | is | you | open | need

_____

3. it. | we | are | When | our | quality, | we | high | mean | say | products

_____

4. get | overtime. | money | extra | I | every | month | if | I | work

_____

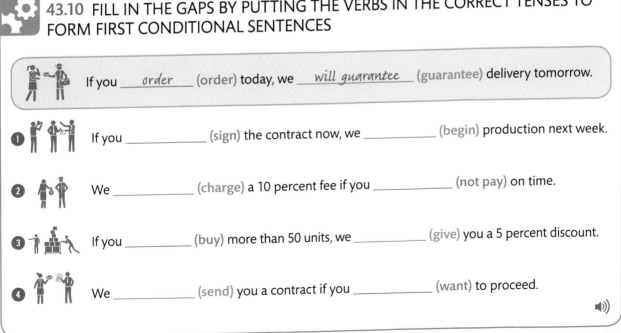

43.10 FILL IN THE GAPS BY PUTTING THE VERBS IN THE CORRECT TENSES TO FORM FIRST CONDITIONAL SENTENCES

If you ____order____ (order) today, we ____will guarantee____ (guarantee) delivery tomorrow.

1. If you _____ (sign) the contract now, we _____ (begin) production next week.

2. We _____ (charge) a 10 percent fee if you _____ (not pay) on time.

3. If you _____ (buy) more than 50 units, we _____ (give) you a 5 percent discount.

4. We _____ (send) you a contract if you _____ (want) to proceed.

43.11 KEY LANGUAGE ZERO, FIRST, AND SECOND CONDITIONALS OVERVIEW

ZERO CONDITIONAL

Use the zero conditional to talk about general truths and things that always happen.

If employees are friendly to clients, they get better tips.

FIRST CONDITIONAL

Use the first conditional to talk about things that are likely to happen.

If Lisa's meeting goes well, she will get a raise.

SECOND CONDITIONAL

Use the second conditional to talk about things that are unlikely to happen, but are still possible.

If Ethan was more polite to clients, he would be promoted.

🔊

 43.12 MATCH THE BEGINNINGS OF THE SENTENCES TO THE CORRECT ENDINGS

If a customer makes a complaint, ————→ we always take it seriously.

if you leave a message.

1. We will return your call ASAP

if our products were more popular there.

2. We would open stores in the US

3. If you need more training,

if we had more staff.

4. We would increase production

if you return your product within 28 days.

5. We will issue a full refund

you can contact the HR department.

🔊

172

43.13 READ THE WEB PAGE AND WRITE ANSWERS TO THE QUESTIONS AS FULL SENTENCES

Business Tips

HOME | ENTRIES | ABOUT | CONTACT

EFFECTIVE NEGOTIATION

Many businesspeople are required to handle negotiations, but few receive any training in how to do it. Here are my top negotiating tips.

Before negotiating
- Do your research. Find out about your business partner. If you understand the other party, you'll understand his or her strengths and weaknesses.
- Before the meeting, decide what you can compromise on. For example, if your business partner offered you Deal A, would you accept it? If not, what would you accept?

During the negotiation
- If you haven't met your business partner before, hold the meeting face to face. Research has shown that meetings in person help to build rapport, so the other party will be more likely to meet you halfway.
- Don't talk more than is necessary. If you talk too much, you run the risk of revealing information that could be useful to the other party.
- Remember, if you keep the meeting professional and listen to each other, you'll reach the goal of any negotiation: finding common ground so that you can reach an agreement and close the deal.

Why might you need negotiation advice?
Few businesspeople are trained to negotiate.

❶ Why should you understand the other party?

_____

❷ What should you decide before negotiating?

_____

❸ Why are face-to-face meetings important?

_____

❹ Why shouldn't you talk too much?

_____

❺ What is the goal of any negotiation?

_____

---

43 ✅ **CHECKLIST**

⚙ Conditionals ☐   **Aa** Negotiating and bargaining ☐   🧩 Discussing possibilities ☐

44 Discussing problems

English uses the third conditional to talk about an unreal past, or events that did not happen. This is useful for talking about workplace mistakes.

⚙ **New language** Third conditional
Aa Vocabulary Workplace mistakes
🧩 **New skill** Talking about past mistakes

44.1 KEY LANGUAGE THE THIRD CONDITIONAL

In third conditional sentences, the past perfect describes something that did not happen, and the "would" clause describes the unreal result.

If you **had paid on time,** we **would have sent the goods to you.**
‌ ‌ ‌ ‌ Past perfect ‌ ‌ ‌ ‌ ‌ ‌ ‌ ‌ ‌ ‌ ‌ ‌ ‌ Past participle

44.2 HOW TO FORM THE THIRD CONDITIONAL

"IF"	PAST PERFECT	REST OF CLAUSE	"WOULD" + "HAVE" + PAST PARTICIPLE	REST OF SENTENCE
If	you had paid	on time,	we would have sent	the goods.

44.3 FURTHER EXAMPLES THE THIRD CONDITIONAL

Third conditional sentences can start with the result.

I wouldn't have missed **the meeting if I** had left **earlier.**

The third conditional can use the short form of "had."

If you'd checked **your work, the clients** wouldn't have **complained.**

If we had wanted **a smaller model,** we would have asked **for one.**

If your staff hadn't been **so rude, we** would have signed **the contract.**

44.4 FILL IN THE GAPS BY PUTTING THE VERBS IN THE CORRECT FORMS TO MAKE THIRD CONDITIONAL SENTENCES

If you ___had spoken___ (speak) more calmly, people ___would have listened___ (listen) to you.

1 If he _____ (use) the correct figures, his report _____ (not be) so out of date.

2 The boss _____ (not shout) if you _____ (admit) your mistake earlier.

3 If you _____ (run) a spell check, the report _____ (not contain) so many errors.

4 We _____ (not embarrass) ourselves if we _____ (research) local customs before our trip.

5 I _____ (work) late last night if I _____ (know) our deadline was so soon.

🔊

44.5 LISTEN TO THE AUDIO AND MARK WHICH THINGS ACTUALLY HAPPENED

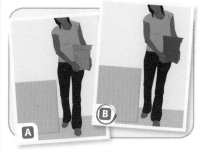

1

2

3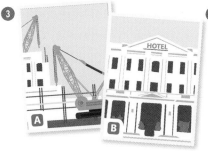

4

5

44.6 KEY LANGUAGE FIRST CONDITIONAL WITH "UNLESS"

You can use "unless" instead of "if...not" in first conditional sentences. In sentences with "unless," the result only happens if the action does not take place.

We will cancel the contract { if you don't / unless you } **repair the copier tomorrow.**

Result ⤸   Action ⤸

44.7 FURTHER EXAMPLES FIRST CONDITIONAL WITH "UNLESS"

We won't be able to offer you a discount unless you order more units.

Elena will get a verbal warning unless her work improves.

44.8 REWRITE THE SENTENCES USING "UNLESS"

If you don't place the order before 3pm, we won't be able to deliver tomorrow.
Unless you place the order before 3pm, we won't be able to deliver tomorrow.

❶ Tony is not going to meet the deadline if he doesn't work overtime.

_____

❷ If I don't get a good performance review, I won't get a raise this year.

_____

❸ I'm afraid we can't track your order if you can't give us your customer reference number.

_____

❹ If we can't offer a better price, we won't win the contract.

_____

44.9 READ THE REPORT AND ANSWER THE QUESTIONS

Customer response to the product was as expected.
True ☐ **False** ☐ **Not given** ☑

❶ Avatar has been a competitor for a long time.
True ☐ **False** ☐ **Not given** ☐

❷ It was known when Avatar would launch its product.
True ☐ **False** ☐ **Not given** ☐

❸ Vivo knew how much Avatar's watch cost.
True ☐ **False** ☐ **Not given** ☐

❹ The Avatar watch is cheaper than the Vivo watch.
True ☐ **False** ☐ **Not given** ☐

❺ The new watch will be ready in six months.
True ☐ **False** ☐ **Not given** ☐

VIVO PRODUCT LAUNCH REPORT

Six months ago we launched our new smartwatch, the Vivo. Sales have been very disappointing and interest in the product is low.

WHY?

Our main competitor, Avatar, launched its new smartwatch one week after us. If we had known this, we would have launched our product later. Furthermore, they priced their smartwatch $50 lower than our product. We would have priced our watch lower if we had known about their competitive price.

WHAT NOW?

Unless we reduce the price of our product to match Avatar's watch, we won't make many sales. I suggest we reduce the price to $125. Furthermore, we need to develop a new, better product. We won't beat Avatar unless we can offer a more functional, better-looking watch.

44 ✔ CHECKLIST

⚙ Third conditional ☐   **Aa** Workplace mistakes ☐   Talking about past mistakes ☐

♻ REVIEW THE ENGLISH YOU HAVE LEARNED IN UNITS 41–44

NEW LANGUAGE	SAMPLE SENTENCE	☑	UNIT
INDIRECT QUESTIONS	Could you tell me **when my order will be ready?**	☐	41.4
THE PASSIVE VOICE FOR POLITENESS	**It seems that a mistake** has been made.	☐	41.9
EMPHASIZING YOUR OPINION	What we need is **an assurance from you about the future.**	☐	42.1
SECOND CONDITIONAL	If you lowered **the price,** I would order **more units.**	☐	43.1
THIRD CONDITIONAL	If you had paid **on time,** we would have delivered **the goods.**	☐	44.1
FIRST CONDITIONAL WITH "UNLESS"	**We will cancel the contract** unless **you repair the copier tomorrow.**	☐	44.6

Answers

1.2 🔊
① Hi, Katherine. I think I **met you at the Market Max conference**.
② I'm not sure whether you **have met each other before**.
③ Yes, we met in Barcelona. **It's great to see you again.**
④ You must be Gloria from the design team. **Guvan told me about your great work.**
⑤ This is Brian from customer services. **Brian, meet Tonya. She's joining our team.**

1.3 🔊
① Did we **meet** at a conference?
② Really good to **see** you again.
③ Roula, meet Maria, **our** new assistant.
④ I'd like to **introduce** you to Karl.
⑤ Have you two **met** each other before?

1.4
① False ② True ③ Not given
④ Not given ⑤ True

1.6
① Shy
② Good ones
③ Ex-colleagues
④ Say sorry
⑤ Unprofessional
⑥ Their eyes
⑦ Your business card

1.7 🔊
① Hi James. I'm Vanisha. I don't think **we've met** before.
② Ashley, I'd like **to** introduce you to my colleague Neil.
③ I **am** enjoying the presentations. Are you?
④ Nice to meet you Bethany. How do you **do**?

1.8 🔊
① Hello Frank. **Are you enjoying** the conference?
② Wilfred, I'd like you to **meet** Roger, our new press officer.

③ Serena, it's really great to **see** you again after so long.
④ I usually enjoy workshops, but I am not finding this one interesting.

2.3 🔊
① They **were beginning** to sell more when the shop suddenly closed last year.
② I **lost** my job when the factory closed last December.
③ I was delighted when I **got** promoted to senior manager in 2015.
④ We moved here when my wife **found** a new job two years ago.
⑤ I **was training** to be a chef when I was given this award.
⑥ When I worked 90 hours a week, I **felt** exhausted all the time.
⑦ When I was a photographer, I **met** a lot of famous people through my work.

2.5 🔊
① I was looking for another job.
② I was wondering if you could help.
③ Were you working as a waiter?
④ They weren't employing young people.
⑤ I didn't enjoy my last job.
⑥ Did you work in a hotel?

2.8 🔊
① He **has taken** 15 days off sick this year and it is only May!
② Julia has a lot of experience. She **has managed** this department for years.
③ They **have employed** more than 300 people over the years.
④ John **has trained** lots of young employees across a few different teams.
⑤ I'm so happy! I **have finished** my apprenticeship at last.
⑥ My manager **has approved** my vacation days. I'm going to Italy in July.

2.9 🔊
① True ② False ③ Not given
④ True ⑤ Not given

2.10 🔊
① I **was driving** taxis when I saw this job advertised.
② I **have managed** accounts for this company for seven years.
③ I **bought** my first business in 2009.
④ I was studying in college when I **saw** this job.
⑤ They **have invested** in this company since 2010.
⑥ In 2014, I sold the company to an investor.

4.3 🔊
① I used to travel to work by car.
② She's used to giving big presentations.
③ I'll get used to my new job eventually.
④ We didn't use to get paid a bonus.
⑤ Did he use to work in marketing?

4.4
Ⓐ 2 Ⓑ 1 Ⓒ 4 Ⓓ 3

4.5 🔊
① We used to finish at noon on Fridays.
② She didn't use to be so serious.
③ I am used to working for a strict boss.
④ Did you use to work in London?

4.6 🔊
① I got used to long hours in my first job.
② He didn't use to have a law degree.
③ I am used to working long hours.
④ You didn't use to work such long hours.
⑤ Did he use to work in a bank?

4.7
① True ② Not given ③ False ④ False
⑤ True

4.8 🔊
① I'm not used to starting at 6am!
② Yes, what a disappointment!
③ Yes, please. It looks delicious.
④ That's a very short commute!
⑤ Yes, I think it's going to rain.

4.9 🔊
① When I was young, I **didn't use to** like mushrooms.
② My grandfather **used to** walk four miles to school every morning.
③ Are you **used to** your new job yet?
④ I grew up in Florida, so I **am used to** the heat.
⑤ We **used to** go to the south of France every year.

05

5.3 🔊
① We have got to ask **for some support on this project**.
② You must put the finished **proposal on my desk tomorrow**.
③ We must not forget **to look after this project while he's away**.
④ I have to help Sami produce **a report about recycling**.
⑤ You don't have **to complete it today**.

5.4 🔊
① We need to increase sales to Europe.
② We can't reveal our new product yet.
③ You don't have to work late.
④ I will need the accounts by tomorrow.
⑤ We have got to find a new IT manager.
⑥ You need to produce a spreadsheet.
⑦ We must reach our sales target.

5.5
① True ② False ③ False ④ False
⑤ Not given

5.7 🔊
① Could you answer my phone?
② Would you call the supplier?
③ We have to finish today.
④ Would you book a meeting?
⑤ Could you send this today?

5.8 🔊
① **Could** you deliver this letter for me, please?
② **Would** you show the new employee around the office?
③ Jess, I **need to** leave early today. Could you let Philippe know?

5.9
① Not given ② True ③ True
④ Not given ⑤ True

07

7.4 🔊
① We **changed** our logo because a lot of people **had complained** about it.
② Some of our goods **had arrived** broken, so we **asked** for a refund.
③ There **were** problems in the warehouse because our manager **had resigned**.
④ Sales of umbrellas **were** poor because we **had had** a dry summer.
⑤ Our clients **were not** happy because we **had missed** our deadline.
⑥ Yasmin's presentation **had gone** very well, so I **gave** her a promotion.
⑦ Our sales **increased** because we **had launched** a new product range.

7.5
②

7.7 🔊
① The purpose of this report is **to** review our sales figures for the last quarter.
② Our **principal** recommendation is to complete the sale of the downtown store.
③ The **following** report presents the results of extensive customer satisfaction research.
④ Our main client **stated** that the recent changes were beneficial for his business.

7.8 🔊
① As can be seen in the table, **the figures for this period were excellent**.
② It is clear from the research **that there were a number of problems**.
③ A number of focus groups **were consulted for this report**.
④ The purpose of this report is **to present the findings of our survey**.

7.9 🔊
① The focus group clients had all **used** both the original and new products.
② The following chart **compares** the sales figures for the two periods.

③ We **asked** the customers who had complained why they didn't like the change.
④ The **purpose** of this report is to present the results of our online trial.
⑤ We started this online trial after our store costs had **risen** by 10 percent.

08

8.2 🔊
① Yes, we'll give you a full refund.
② Yes, it's AMLGW14.
③ OK. No problem.
④ Our courier has been having difficulties.
⑤ I'm very sorry to hear that, Mrs. Singh.
⑥ Yes, we'll send you a new one tomorrow.

8.3
Ⓐ 3 Ⓑ 1 Ⓒ 6 Ⓓ 5 Ⓔ 2 Ⓕ 4

8.4 🔊
① We'll **look** into the problem for you.
② We'll **give** you a discount voucher.
③ Could you hold the **line** a moment?
④ Let's see **what** we can do.

8.8 🔊
① The customers **have been waiting** for us to contact them.
② Our engineers **have been working** on the line for two days.
③ What **have** you **been doing** to solve the problem?
④ I **have been watching** your program and I want to complain.
⑤ We **have been repairing** the broken cables this morning.
⑥ They **have been updating** my software and now it doesn't work.

8.9
① True
② Not given
③ True
④ False
⑤ Not given

10

10.2
③

10.3 🔊
① I just wanted to **check** that you will be able to make it to the meeting.
② Don't worry if you have any questions. Just let me **know**.
③ I'm **copying** Maxine in on this as she may have some more information.
④ How **about** coming to the restaurant with us this evening?
⑤ I was **wondering** if you and Ana could come to the meeting tomorrow.
⑥ Give me a call if you can't **make** the presentation at 10 o'clock

11

11.2
① Present ② Future
③ Future ④ Present

11.3 Model Answers
① The delivery van was involved in an accident yesterday.
② The company is receiving new stock tomorrow.
③ She is hoping to confirm a new delivery date next week.
④ She can cancel her order online.
⑤ Yasmin should contact Janice if she has any questions.

11.4 🔊
① to hesitate
② to prefer
③ to obtain
④ to confirm
⑤ to inform
⑥ to contact
⑦ to request

11.6 🔊
① I am hoping
② We are currently waiting
③ we are expecting
④ I was wondering
⑤ I assure you
⑥ We will be doing
⑦ please do not hesitate to contact me

11.7 🔊
① I was **wondering** if you would meet the clients at their factory.
② We **are** having difficulties with deliveries due to the weather.
③ Will you be **paying** for the order by bank transfer or credit card?
④ We are aiming **to** finish the redecorating by next Wednesday.

11.8 🔊
① We are still waiting to hear from our supplier.
② I was wondering if you could call me back.
③ Will you be attending the progress meeting next week?

12

12.3 🔊
① I'll look **into** the problem now.
② The printer has run **out** of ink.
③ I need to **catch** up with you.
④ Sorry, I have to hang **up** now.
⑤ Could you deal **with** this order?
⑥ I'll **look** into Mr. Li's query.
⑦ My client just hung **up** on me!

12.4
Ⓐ 6 Ⓑ 3 Ⓒ 5 Ⓓ 1 Ⓔ 2 Ⓕ 4

12.5 🔊
① bring up
② turn up
③ chill out
④ fill out
⑤ figure out

12.8 🔊
① James, can you **pass on** the message to Zane?
② Welcome to Jo's. Please **fill** the visitor's form **out**.
③ Can you stand at the exit and **hand** the leaflets **out**?
④ **Put** a helmet **on** before entering the site.
⑤ Before I update the software, **back** your files **up**.

12.9 🔊
① Could you please **pass** the message **on** to Gary?
② I have an important meeting, so I **put** a suit **on** this morning.
③ Howard, we should really **fix** a meeting **up** for this week.
④ After a busy day in the office, I usually **chill out** at home.

14

14.2
① True ② False ③ False ④ Not given
⑤ False

14.3 🔊
① Over the last year, an exciting new line has been **developed**.
② This design **was** patented in 1938. Nobody has ever managed to make a better product!
③ Their new line **is being** launched next Saturday. Everyone is talking about it.
④ Our factory floor **was** cleaned before the CEO visited. He was happy things looked good!
⑤ You don't need to worry about dinner. The food **is** cooked to order so that it is fresh.
⑥ The first cars made in this factory **were** sold in the UK in 1972, and worldwide the next year.
⑦ Our original designers **were** influenced by Japanese artists.
⑧ To prepare for the launch, advertising posters **are being** put up around town as we speak.

14.6

1 Their new products **are being promoted** on TV now.
2 80,000 packets **are produced** in the factory each week.
3 A thousand new cars **will be sold** next week.
4 Our latest gadget **was invented** by Ronnie Angel.
5 The production line **is stopped** during the summer.
6 Great advances in design **have been made** recently.

14.7

1 All the cars are checked by someone before they leave the factory.
2 The new photo app for professional artists was invented by Maxine.
3 All Carl Osric's books were bought by customers on the publication date.
4 All our vegetarian ingredients are bought from the market by Ron.
5 All of the invoices are checked by Samantha before they are sent out.

14.8

Ⓐ 3 Ⓑ 1 Ⓒ 6 Ⓓ 2 Ⓔ 7 Ⓕ 8 Ⓖ 4
Ⓗ 5

14.10

1 These flowers must have been bought today.
2 They can't be marked down yet! They're new.
3 This picture couldn't have been drawn by Sanjit.
4 The price shouldn't have been accepted.
5 These glasses must be packaged carefully.
6 Faults in the product shouldn't be ignored.
7 The oven has been turned up.

14.11

1 The chassis parts are placed on the **assembly line**.
2 The engine and radiator **are lifted** by a robot as they are very heavy.
3 The engine and radiator **are secured** to the chassis by an assembly worker.
4 The bodywork is fully **assembled and welded** on a separate line.

5 The assembled bodywork is inspected before **being painted** by a robot.
6 The chassis and bodywork are joined together before the vehicle **is checked**.

15

15.3

OPINION: **awesome**, **awful**
SIZE: **enormous**, **tiny**
AGE: **modern**, **out-dated**
COLOR: **green**, **red**
NATIONALITY: **Swiss**, **Indian**
MATERIAL: **wooden**, **fabric**

15.4

1 Have you seen the ugly, plastic desks?
2 We're launching the new, metallic range tomorrow.
3 Would you prefer these tiny, diamond ones?

15.5

1 B 2 A 3 A 4 A 5 B

15.7

1 I'm interested in that **incredible** modern device we saw at the sales fair.
2 Our competitors are still selling those really **ugly**, large cotton shirts.
3 The office has a **friendly**, old black cat that visits regularly.
4 Frances, have you seen these Peruvian **silver** earrings that I brought back?
5 Did you get one of those new **plastic** business cards?
6 A lot of customers have been asking for the **new** red version.
7 My boss has asked me to design a small, **paper** package for the product.
8 I have bought some new **leather** chairs for the boardroom.

15.8

1 True
2 Not given
3 False
4 False
5 False

15.9

1 We offer great, **delicious** food that people can afford.
2 Look at that **enormous** new billboard across the street.
3 I love buying **antique** wooden furniture for the office.
4 My boss drives a tiny **green** car to work. It's definitely easy to spot!
5 We aim to offer awesome, **friendly** customer service at all times.

17

17.3

EXTREME:
awful, **fantastic**, **tiny**, **disgusting**, **enormous**
ABSOLUTE:
unique, **impossible**, **right**, **perfect**, **wrong**
CLASSIFYING:
organic, **digital**, **industrial**, **electronic**, **chemical**

17.4

1 True
2 True
3 Not given
4 False
5 False
6 Not given

17.7

1 The new gadget is completely digital.
2 This draft design is practically perfect.
3 The client said it was totally fantastic.
4 His decision to invest was entirely right.
5 This area of town is largely industrial.

17.9

1 mainly European
2 pretty confident
3 absolutely delicious

18.2 🔊
❶ Is the office big enough for us?
❷ The delivery times are too slow.
❸ Are these shelves strong enough?

18.3
❶ B ❷ A ❸ A ❹ A ❺ B

18.4
❶ False
❷ True
❸ Not given
❹ True
❺ False

18.6 🔊
❶ It's such a great product.
❷ The meeting was so boring.
❸ His news was such a surprise.
❹ My boss is so ambitious.
❺ Their phones are so cheap.
❻ Her company is so big!
❼ Our launch was such a surprise!

18.7 🔊
❶ The slogan is far **too** complicated.
We need to simplify it.
❷ They have created **such** a brilliant
poster campaign.
❸ We haven't done **enough** market
research. We need to understand our
consumers.
❹ Our supervisor is **such** a creative person.
She designed our new logo.
❺ Marion is **so** persuasive when she delivers
a sales pitch.

19.3 🔊
❶ You must tell your boss it will be late.
❷ You shouldn't start work so early.
❸ You shouldn't work such long shifts.
❹ You should take a walk outside right now.

19.4 🔊
❶ My wife said I **could try** yoga and
relaxation techniques.
❷ You **should stop** working right away
if you feel sick.
❸ You **ought to take** a break if you're
really tired.
❹ You **shouldn't feel** exhausted at the
beginning of the week.
❺ You **must delegate** some of your work
to your assistant.

19.5 🔊
❶ You **ought to** relax more.
❷ You **must stop** taking work home
every day.
❸ He **could try** to delegate more tasks.
❹ You **shouldn't worry** so much
about work.
❺ She **should talk** to her colleagues.
❻ He **ought to quit** his job if he hates it.

19.6
❶ No ❷ Yes ❸ Yes ❹ Yes

19.10 🔊
1. What about taking a break?
2. What about buying better equipment?
3. What about training new employees?
4. Why don't we take a break?
5. Why don't we buy better equipment?
6. Why don't we train new employees?

19.11 🔊
❶ Why don't we **buy** new chairs?
❷ Why don't we **go** for a walk outside?
❸ What about **drinking** less coffee?
❹ Why don't we **provide** free fruit?
❺ What about **making** a list of your tasks?
❻ What about **delegating** this to Jo?
❼ Why don't we **ask** Paul to help us?

19.12
❶ True
❷ False
❸ True
❹ False
❺ True
❻ False

21.3 🔊
❶ She doesn't like meeting new people.
She **can't** work in the HR department.
❷ Shaun **can** work really well with new
employees, so he should help run our
training course.
❸ Have you seen her brilliant photographs?
She **can** create our posters and flyers.
❹ Lydia failed her driving test, so,
unfortunately, she **can't** drive the
delivery van.

21.5 🔊
❶ Peter **couldn't** use the new coffee
machine. He didn't know how it worked.
❷ Varinder **couldn't** write reports very
well at first, but she can now that she's had
more practice.
❸ No one in the office **could** read his
handwriting. It was awful.
❹ Bill was the only person who **couldn't**
figure out how to use the photocopier.

21.7 🔊
❶ Future
❷ Past
❸ Future
❹ Past
❺ Future

21.8
❶ True
❷ Not given
❸ True
❹ False
❺ False

21.9 🔊
❶ James's team was weak, but he's trained
them well and now they **can** do anything.
❷ We think that you are really creative and
would make a great addition to the PR team.
❸ I don't know what is wrong with me
today. I **can't** get anything finished.
❹ My confidence is much better now.
Before, I **couldn't** talk in public.

22.3 ◀))
❶ **Although** I attended the training session, I'm not sure I learned very much.
❷ You got a high score for the IT test, and you've done **equally** well on the team-building course.
❸ Team A built a small boat out of plastic bottles, **whereas** Team B used wood to make theirs.
❹ The training day is a great way to learn new skills. It's **also** a good way to get to know people.

22.4
❶ Walked across bridges high in the air
❷ Overcome fear and help each other
❸ The tallest and the most scared
❹ Disagreed with each other
❺ Work more slowly and listen to their teammates

22.6 ◀))
❶ The course taught us how to lead a team. As a consequence, I feel more confident.
❷ I'd never ridden a horse before. For this reason, I was quite scared during the training.
❸ Team Lion completed the challenge first. Consequently, they all received medals.

22.7 ◀))
❶ Team A had to build a cardboard tower, **while Team B had to bake a cake**.
❷ Although I liked going to the beach, **I didn't enjoy swimming in the ocean**.
❸ I love learning new things. **As a result, I really enjoyed the training day**.
❹ Team building is a good way to learn new skills **and it's also a chance to relax**.

22.8
❶ Not given ❷ True ❸ False
❹ Not given ❺ True

22.9 ◀))
Model Answers
❶ This course will teach you new skills. It will help you to get to know each other, **too**.
❷ **Although** Team B completed the task first, they had some major communication problems.

❸ By doing this task, we'll not only identify the team's weaknesses, but **also** its strengths.
❹ Team A worked together very well. Team B were **equally** cooperative.

23.4 ◀))
❶ Mara has offered **to organize** the accommodation for our guests.
❷ I keep **suggesting** that our company should organize a golf day, but my boss disagrees.
❸ We like **to offer** our clients a wide range of food at our conferences.
❹ I enjoy **helping** out at company open days because I get to meet lots of people.
❺ Before I start planning, I usually make a list of all the customers I want **to invite**.
❻ I expect **to stay** late tonight to help Martina decorate the conference hall.

23.5
Model Answers
❶ The SmartTech Fair opened in 1987.
❷ It is helping us to live healthier lives.
❸ They could shape the future of the car industry.
❹ You can register your interest online.
❺ You can buy tickets from the SmartTech website.

23.8 ◀))
❶ We stopped holding breakfast meetings **because few people attended them**.
❷ We regret to announce **that there will be some job losses**.
❸ I'm sure Shona will remember **to book the conference room**.
❹ Sahib went on working **until midnight in order to finish the report**.

23.9
❶ False
❷ Not given
❸ False
❹ Not given
❺ True
❻ True

23.10 ◀))
1. I remember meeting him in Tokyo.
2. I was supposed to book a nice hotel room.
3. I wanted to book a nice hotel room.
4. She was supposed to book a nice hotel room.
5. She wanted to book a nice hotel room.
6. We remember meeting him in Tokyo.
7. We wanted to book a nice hotel room.
8. They remember meeting him in Tokyo.
9. They wanted to book a nice hotel room.

23.14 ◀))
❶ My boss asked me **to arrange** a meeting with our clients.
❷ Our clients **asked us** to visit them in Paris.
❸ We expect all our staff **to arrive** on time.
❹ We **invited all our clients** to attend our end-of-year party.
❺ I expect my manager **to give** me a promotion soon.

23.15 ◀))
❶ Our clients expect to receive excellent service.
❷ My boss invited me to attend a conference.
❸ My business degree allowed me to get this job.

25.4 ◀))
❶ She said she paid the invoice.
❷ He said he would pay the invoice.
❸ He said he would arrange a meeting.
❹ He said he was arranging a meeting.
❺ She said she had finished writing the report.
❻ She said she would finish writing the report.

25.5 ◀))
❶ She **said (that) she would interview the candidates**.
❷ He **said (that) he met the CEO on Monday**. / He **said (that) he'd met the CEO on Monday**.
❸ He **said (that) he could book the meeting room**.

④ She **said (that) she was writing a press release**.
⑤ He **said (that) he could use design software**.

25.8
Ⓐ 2　Ⓑ 4　Ⓒ 5　Ⓓ 1　Ⓔ 3

25.10 ◄))
① She said that she didn't understand the email.
② He said there was a problem with his computer.
③ She said we need to reply to those customers.

25.14 ◄))
① Sharon **confirmed** that the sales figures would be ready by 5pm.
② Lilia **promised** that she would stay late to help me finish the report.
③ Mr. Lee **announced** that we had beaten our sales target for the year.
④ Ben **complained** that the coffee from the machine tasted awful.
⑤ She **suggested** that I could ask my boss about a raise.

26

26.4 ◄))
① He asked me why I was late again.
② Lara asked me where the meeting was.
③ She asked me why I had missed the interview.
④ He asked me who had taken the minutes.

26.5
① True　② False　③ True　④ Not given
⑤ True　⑥ False　⑦ Not given

26.6
① Not given　② False　③ True　④ Not given　⑤ False　⑥ Not given

26.7 ◄))
① The boss is angry with Max. He told him to **do his work** before he leaves.
② Mr. Tan promised that I would **get promoted** to manager if I worked hard.

③ Could you **do me a favor**? Could you make 20 copies of this, please?
④ Can I **make a suggestion**? Finish the proposal first, then work on the spreadsheet.
⑤ Paola said that she usually **gets home** from work at 6:30pm.
⑥ Paul said that he **had an appointment** with his boss, but he was really late.

26.9 ◄))
Model Answers
① She asked (me) what the consumer feedback was.
② He asked (me) whether I had a strategy. / He asked (me) if I had a strategy.
③ She asked (me) who was getting promoted.
④ He asked (me) what the main points were.
⑤ She asked (me) if he was the new marketing manager. / She asked (me) whether he was the new marketing manager.

27

27.2 ◄))
① We'll have to reduce the price. Very few customers have bought our new jeans.
② So few people pay by check these days that we no longer accept this form of payment.
③ Unfortunately, we've had few inquiries about our new spa treatments.

27.4 ◄))
① Unfortunately, there is **little** chance of us winning this contract.
② I have **a few** ideas that I really think could improve our brand image.
③ There is still **a little** time left before we need to submit the report.
④ Kelvin has **little** understanding of accountancy.
⑤ So **few** people have bought this TV that we're going to stop production.

27.6 ◄))
① All you can do is apologize for your mistake.
② All I expect is for staff to complete their tasks.

③ I'm sure all will be well in the interview.
④ All I want is a raise.
⑤ We have all the information we need.

27.7 ◄))
① The only thing we need is a photo.
② We have some money.
③ We have some time.
④ Not many people like Mr. Jenkins.
⑤ Bertha is an expert in IT.
⑥ Some people like Mr. Jenkins.
⑦ We don't have much time.

27.8
① Not given　② False　③ True　④ True
⑤ False　⑥ False

28

28.4 ◄))
① Who is the manager?
② What's in the report?
③ Who answers the telephone?
④ Who approves annual vacation?
⑤ What is the deadline?
⑥ Who wrote the ad?
⑦ Who will take questions?
⑧ What are the objectives?
⑨ What's the complaint about?

28.5 ◄))
① What are our most popular products?
② Do you need to book the meeting?
③ Who answers customer emails?
④ Did Savannah write this report?
⑤ What is our lowest price?
⑥ Is James on vacation next week?

28.8 ◄))
① You haven't read my proposal, **have you**?
② Sean could give the presentation, **couldn't he**?
③ Zoe got promoted, **didn't she**?
④ We're not ready for the conference, **are we**?
⑤ You work in marketing, **don't you**?

28.9 🔊
1. Alice would know the answer, **wouldn't she**?
2. I'm not dressed formally enough, **am I**?
3. You've worked in Berlin, **haven't you**?
4. They could tell us before 6pm, **couldn't they**?
5. Kate's going to Bangkok, **isn't she**?
6. I should double check the figures, **shouldn't I**?
7. Richard didn't get a raise, **did he**?

28.11
1. Not given 2. False 3. False 4. True
5. True

28.12 🔊
1. What was the name of the company? I didn't **hear**.
2. **Who** is working on the project for the new office?
3. You identified the mistake, **didn't you**?
4. Could you repeat that, please? I didn't **catch** it.
5. **What** is the theme of this year's conference?

30

30.2 🔊
1. **The** deadline for applications is Friday.
2. This job is based in **the** Berlin office.
3. We are recruiting **a** new designer.
4. I've got **an** interview for a new job.
5. **The** application form for this job is long.
6. Please complete **the** form on our website.
7. **The** ideal candidate enjoys teamwork.
8. There's an ad for **an** English teacher.

30.3
Ⓐ 2 Ⓑ 1 Ⓒ 4 Ⓓ 3 Ⓔ 5

30.6 🔊
1. The jobs I'm really interested in are based in Los Angeles. They're in IT.
2. The people who interviewed me for the job were really nice. They were the managers.
3. Clients can be very demanding. The clients I met today had lots of complaints.

30.9 🔊
1. I often travel to **Hong Kong** on business.
2. **Zenith Accounting** has three job openings.
3. I have a meeting with **the company director**.
4. He works for **the World Health Organization**.
5. I'm a strong candidate because I speak **Russian**.

30.10
1. Europe
2. an opening
3. Flight attendants
4. The hours
5. build a career

30.11 🔊
1. Your meeting is with **the HR manager**.
2. We're recruiting more staff in **France**.
3. I'm looking for a job as **an education consultant**.
4. We need someone who can speak **Italian**.
5. **Omnitech** is advertising several vacancies in its marketing department.
6. I work in **the sales department** of a large company.

31

31.3 🔊
1. In our department, we focus **on** sales and marketing.
2. Katrina graduated **from** college with a degree in Biological Sciences.
3. Our technicians are fully trained **in** all aspects of health and safety.
4. I've applied **for** a job in the IT department of a big company in Los Angeles.

31.4
1. Not given
2. Not given
3. True
4. False
5. True
6. True

31.5 🔊
1. to be responsible for something
2. to look forward to something
3. to amount to
4. to apply for a job
5. to be passionate about
6. experience in something

31.8 🔊
1. When can I expect to hear **from** you about the job?
2. Unfortunately, there has been a rise **in** complaints from customers.
3. I work **for** the CEO of a big IT company. I'm her assistant.
4. I heard **about** the job through a friend who works at the company.
5. Our profits went up last year. There was a rise **of** about five percent.

31.9
1. résumé
2. reliable
3. team
4. skills
5. salary
6. referee

31.10
Dear Mr. Khan,

I am writing to **apply for** the **position** of head web designer with your company.

I have **experience in** managing large commercial websites. Last year, sales from the website that I designed for a major online store **amounted to** more than $6 million.

I am eager to develop my **skills** and broaden my knowledge of other **industries**. I believe this job would be a fantastic **opportunity** for me, and I'd add a great deal to your company. I am enthusiastic and **passionate about** being at the cutting edge of web development. I'm also very **reliable** and I enjoy working in a team.

I have attached my **résumé** and details of my referees. I look forward to **hearing from** you.

Yours sincerely,
Amy Quah

32.2 🔊
1 The office that I work in **is modern and open-plan**.
2 The customers who gave us **feedback were all very positive**.
3 One thing that I don't like **about my job is the long hours**.
4 The people who are on my team **say they enjoy working with me**.
5 The product that we've just launched **is already selling very well**.

32.3 🔊
1 The main thing **that** I hope to gain by working here is more experience.
2 The area **that** I live in is very close to the bus routes into the business district.
3 The tasks **that** I perform best usually involve customer relations.
4 The exams **that** I passed last year mean that I am now fully qualified.
5 The person **who** I have learned the most from is my college professor.
6 The countries **that** order most of our umbrellas are in Europe.
7 The achievement **that** I am most proud of is winning "employee of the year."

32.5 🔊
1 I have completed all the training, **which** means you wouldn't need to train me.
2 My boss, **who** is very talented, always encourages me not to work too late.
3 IT development, **which** is my favorite part of the job, is very fast-paced.
4 My co-workers, who are all older than me, have taught me a lot.
5 I worked at the reception desk, **which** taught me how to deal with customers.
6 I take my job very seriously, which means I always follow the company dress code.
7 In my last job, **which** was in Paris, I learned to speak French fluently.

32.6
Ⓐ 3 Ⓑ 6 Ⓒ 5 Ⓓ 2 Ⓔ 1 Ⓕ 4

32.8 🔊
1 The place **where** I can concentrate the best is at home.
2 The person **whose** career inspires me the most is Muhammad Ali.
3 Last year, **when** I was an intern, I learned how to give presentations.
4 My parents, **who** are both doctors, inspired me to study medicine.

32.9 🔊
1 My current salary, **which is** $20,000 a year, is not very high.
2 The thing **that gets** me excited about my job is seeing our products on sale.
3 Yes. I always know **who has** the responsibility for getting a task done on my team.
4 I can identify things **that need** to change, to make your business more efficient.
5 My boss, **who is** quite flexible, would allow me to leave after six weeks' notice.

34.3 🔊
1 to live up to something
2 to look forward to something
3 to come across as something
4 to get away with something
5 to run out of something
6 to keep up with someone

34.4
1 True 2 Not given 3 False
4 Not given 5 True 6 False

34.5 🔊
1 Please could you **come** up with a proposal on how to improve punctuality?
2 I can't **keep** up with Thom when he goes through the accounts. He's too quick.
3 Liza comes **across** as very serious, but outside of work she's a lot of fun.
4 The two interns don't get **along** with each other very well. They don't see eye to eye.
5 I'm really looking **forward** to welcoming our new clients to London.

34.8 🔊
1 Can you **take it on**?
2 We're **giving them away**.
3 Let's **look it up** on social media.
4 I think we should **call it off**.
5 Can we **talk it over**?

34.9
1 Needs a modern image
2 Advertise the event
3 Increase awareness of the company
4 Tariq volunteers to do it

34.10 🔊
1 I need the report today. Please don't let **me down**.
2 Josef complains a lot. I can't put **up** with it.
3 I'm looking **forward** to finishing my training.
4 If you have a problem, we can talk **it** over.
5 Don't look down **on** Rachel. She's still new.
6 Our company is giving **away** three cars.

35.3 🔊
1 Tanya has used up all her leave.
She won't go on vacation this year.
2 Toby is great at managing people.
He will be promoted to lead his team.
3 Josef doesn't get along with his boss.
He might not stay here much longer.
4 We have some meetings in Japan.
You may have to go to Tokyo.

35.4 🔊
1 We can't hire any staff at the moment, so you might not get an assistant until May.
2 You're great with new staff, so we may ask you to become a mentor.
3 It's been a bad year for the company, so you won't get a raise.
4 This report needs to be finished by Friday. You might need to work overtime.
5 If Lucinda's work doesn't improve, we may have to fire her.

35.5

1 True **2** False **3** True **4** False
5 True **6** False **7** True **8** False

35.7 🔊

1 He **definitely won't** get the job.
2 You probably **won't need** any training.
3 We **will probably hire** some more
staff soon.
4 She **will definitely** get a raise.
5 I **definitely won't** move to the
head office.
6 I **probably won't** go on vacation
this year.

35.8 🔊

1 We will **probably** get a thank-you gift.
2 I **definitely** won't change jobs this year.
3 You will **definitely** get a bonus.
4 We **probably** won't invite him to
the meeting.

35.9

1 may happen
2 might not happen
3 probably won't happen
4 definitely won't happen

37

37.2

1 False **2** True **3** True **4** False
5 Not given

37.3 🔊

1 To sum up, we have a very bright future.
2 Do feel free to ask me any questions.
3 Let's turn to the predicted sales figures.
4 So, we've looked at all the main
alternatives.

37.4 🔊

1 hard drive
2 pointer
3 power button
4 slides
5 cable
6 lectern
7 remote

37.5 🔊

1 Be careful of the **cable** in front of
the stage.
2 I will return to the **lectern** to answer
questions.
3 If you follow my **pointer**, you can see
the graph.
4 I'll use my **remote** to forward to the
final slide.
5 This projector's noisy. I'll turn the **power
button** off.

37.6

1 False **2** Not given **3** True **4** True
5 False **6** False

37.7

A 2 **B** 6 **C** 8 **D** 1 **E** 5 **F** 7 **G** 4
H 3

38

38.2 🔊

GENERALIZING: **on the whole**, **generally**,
in general, **by and large**
EXCEPTIONS: **except for**, **with the
exception of**, **aside from**, **excepting**
FOCUSING: **if we focus on**, **if we home in
on**, **concentrating on**, **focusing on**

38.3 🔊

1 The launch was successful, aside from
the interview.
2 Now, let's home in on the positive news.
3 By and large, the poster campaign was
a disaster.
4 Most of our clients liked the design
except one.
5 Today we're going to focus on
social media.

38.4

1 True **2** Not given **3** False **4** Not
given **5** True

38.7

1 False **2** True **3** True **4** False

38.8 🔊

1 No. **If we focus on** the posters, we can
see they were very successful.
2 Yes, **with the exception of** our
Madrid store.
3 **As a matter of fact** it was very successful.
4 Cities **such as** Seoul and Busan could
have successful stores.
5 They haven't yet. **However**, it's too soon
to see what the impact will be.

39

39.3 🔊

1 Our new smartwatch is **easier** to operate
than the old one.
2 Our new designer jeans are **more** stylish
than last year's products.
3 Our tablet is **the** cheapest on the market.
4 This is the **most** beautiful dress in
our range.
5 This is the **best** laptop I have ever owned.

39.4

1 more comfortable **2** the most reliable
3 lighter **4** more affordable

39.7 🔊

1 Our new phone is as cheap as existing
models, but has a much wider range
of features.
2 Our latest DVD is as exciting as anything
I've ever seen.
3 Our chairs are excellent value, and just as
comfortable as more expensive models.

39.8

1 True **2** Not given **3** False
4 True **5** Not given

39.9 🔊

1 Our new laptop is much **lighter** than
its competitors.
2 This fitness tracker is **just as effective as**
more expensive models.
3 Organic fruit is not **as cheap as**
supermarket fruit, but it tastes better.
4 A consumer survey voted our pizzas the
tastiest on the market.

40.2
Ⓐ 6 Ⓑ 1 Ⓒ 2 Ⓓ 7 Ⓔ 5 Ⓕ 8 Ⓖ 3
Ⓗ 4

40.3 🔊
❶ There was a steady increase in our share value.
❷ Interest in our bags declined considerably.
❸ We've had a sharp rise in customer numbers.
❹ There was a dramatic spike in sales in May.
❺ Sales of our bags have rallied slightly.
❻ The value of our shares has fallen steadily.
❼ The value of the dollar is fluctuating wildly.
❽ The value of the dollar saw a dramatic spike.

40.5 🔊
❶ Returns have increased **by** 10 percent.
❷ Prices fell between 30 **and** 45 percent.
❸ We're shrinking our staff **from** 800 to 650.
❹ Year-end profit stands **at** 8 percent.
❺ Salaries will increase **by** 2 percent.
❻ We have **between** 1,100 and 1,200 staff.
❼ There was a decrease **of** 5 percent.
❽ Profits have fallen **by** 15 percent.
❾ We are lowering the price **to** 30 euros.
❿ The price peaked **at** £19.99.

40.6
❶ False
❷ True
❸ True
❹ Not given

40.7 🔊
❶ There was a **sharp increase** at the start of the year.
❷ It has been **fluctuating wildly** since the announcement.
❸ We're expecting them to **rally considerably** next quarter.

41.2 🔊
❶ Yes, I think we could do that.
❷ We might move forward if we can agree on a delivery date.
❸ Maybe we could consider different colors.
❹ Would you mind waiting until next month for payment?
❺ We were hoping it would be more innovative.

41.3
ⓘ 1,000
❷ It is too high
❸ A cake
❹ Next week

41.7 🔊
❶ I was wondering whether you have these in another size.
❷ Could you tell me when the price list will be ready?
❸ Could you tell me when I can expect delivery?

41.8 🔊
❶ Could you tell me when **I can** start buying the new products?
❷ I was wondering **what the warranty period is**.
❸ Could you tell me how **the new product is** different from the old one?
❹ I was wondering if **you would** be free to discuss a new job opening.

41.10 🔊
❶ Could you tell me whether **the delivery date has been changed**?
❷ I was wondering whether **my invoice has been paid**.
❸ It seems that **the wrong product was sent**.
❹ It looks as if **my complaint was not fully understood**.
❺ It seems that **the price was not calculated correctly**.

41.11 🔊
❶ I'm afraid I can't access **the computer system right now**.
❷ It looks as if **the discount has not been applied**.
❸ I was wondering why the **deadline has been missed**.
❹ Could you tell me when **the sales start**?
❺ It seems that the wrong customer **has been contacted**.

41.12
❶ Not given
❷ True
❸ False
❹ False
❺ Not given

42.3 🔊
❶ If you ask **me**, we might be better to wait until the summer.
❷ **What** we need is proof that your business is profitable.
❸ **Actually**, we'd like to reach an agreement by the end of the day.
❹ The **main** thing is that we agree on a price that everyone is happy with.

42.4
Ⓐ 2
Ⓑ 4
Ⓒ 1
Ⓓ 3
Ⓔ 5

42.5 🔊
❶ Not quite. **What we need are** some references from your customers.
❷ That's OK. The **main thing is that** we find the right person to do the work.
❸ **Actually**, our quote already includes free delivery.

43.4 🔊
1 I would **place** an order if they delivered sooner.
2 If your product **was** cheaper, we would buy it.
3 If you moved the deadline, we **could meet** it.
4 I **would** work with them if they answered my questions.
5 If they **checked** their work, I would use them.

43.5
1 True
2 Not given
3 True
4 False
5 Not given

43.6 🔊
1 We **would sign** the contract if it **was** clearer.
2 I **would accept** the job offer if the pay **was** better.
3 If they **improved** the quality, we **would place** an order.
4 If I **had** more time today, I **would check** the contract.

43.9 🔊
1 If you pay by credit card, we charge a 2 percent fee.
2 Our helpline is open 24 hours a day if you need assistance.
3 When we say our products are high quality, we mean it.
4 I get extra money every month if I work overtime.

43.10 🔊
Note: All answers can also use the short form of the future with "will."
1 If you **sign** the contract now, we **will begin** production next week.
2 We **will charge** a 10 percent fee if you **don't pay / do not pay** on time.
3 If you **buy** more than 50 units, we **will give** you a 5 percent discount.
4 We **will send** you a contract if you **want** to proceed.

43.12 🔊
1 We will return your call ASAP **if you leave a message**.
2 We would open stores in the US **if our products were more popular there**.
3 If you need more training, **you can contact the HR department**.
4 We would increase production **if we had more staff**.
5 We will issue a full refund **if you return your product within 28 days**.

43.13 Model Answers
1 You will understand his or her strengths and weaknesses.
2 You should decide what you can compromise on.
3 They help to build rapport if you don't know your business partner.
4 If you talk too much, you run the risk of revealing useful information.
5 To find a common ground so that you can reach an agreement.

44.4 🔊
Note: All answers can also be written in contracted form.
1 If he **had used** the correct figures, his report **would not have been** so out of date.
2 The boss **would not have shouted** if you **had admitted** your mistake earlier.
3 If you **had run** a spell check, the report **would not have contained** so many errors.
4 We **would not have embarrassed** ourselves if we **had researched** local customs before our trip.
5 I **would have worked** late last night if I **had known** our deadline was so soon.

44.5
1 B
2 A
3 A
4 B
5 A

44.8 🔊
1 Tony is not going to meet the deadline **unless he works overtime**.
2 **Unless I get** a good performance review, I won't get a raise this year.
3 I'm afraid we can't track your order **unless you can** give us your customer reference number.
4 **Unless we can** offer a better price, we won't win the contract.

44.9
1 Not given 2 False 3 False
4 True 5 Not given

Index

Subjects are indexed by unit number. Entries in **bold** indicate the unit with the most information.

Acknowledgments

The publisher would like to thank:
Amy Child, Dominic Clifford, Devika Khosla, and Priyansha Tuli for design assistance; Dominic Clifford and Hansa Babra for additional illustrations; Sam Atkinson, Vineetha Mokkil, Antara Moitra, Margaret Parrish, Nisha Shaw, and Rohan Sinha for editorial assistance;

Elizabeth Wise for indexing; Jo Kent for additional text; Scarlett O'Hara, Georgina Palffy, and Helen Ridge for proofreading; Christine Stroyan for project management; ID Audio for audio recording and production; David Almond, Gillian Reid, and Jacqueline Street-Elkayam for production assistance.

DK would like to thank the following for their kind permission to use their photographs:
71 **Fotolia**: Maksym Dykha (bottom right).
150 **Alamy**: MBI (bottom right).
All other images are copyright DK.
For more information, please visit **www.dkimages.com**.